Confessions of a
First-Year Maestro

A Guide to Your
First Year of Teaching

G-5960

Confessions of a First-Year Maestro

A Guide to Your
First Year of Teaching

Catherine Bell Robertson

GIA Publications, Inc.
Chicago

Confessions of a First-Year Maestro
A Guide to Your First Year of Teaching

Catherine Bell Robertson

Jacket design and illustration by Yolanda Durán
Book design and illustration by Yolanda Durán

G-5960
ISBN: 1-57999-260-9
Copyright © 2003 GIA Publications, Inc.
7404 S. Mason Ave., Chicago, IL 60638
www. giamusic.com
1.800.442.1358
All rights reserved.
Printed in the United States of America.

Table of Contents

foreward
by Tim Lautzenheiser

We are fortunate to have music as part of our school curriculums, and we enjoy a rich tradition of music learning in our schools. Students of music education are required to complete a rigorous slate of music classes as they prepare to enter the profession as a music teacher.

Whether it is four years of university study or four hundred years of classroom training, there is no degree program that offers the needed tools-of-the-trade to properly prepare the first year teacher for what lies ahead. Regardless of talent, academic achievements, or prior successes, the new teacher is certain to experience "baptism by fire."

Reading Kate Robertson's wonderful autobiographical diary is certain to bring a knowing smile to your face and a heartfelt desire to send an empathetic message of reassurance to every rookie teacher. In spite of the tried-and-true advice of our college mentors, the wake up call of reality can be a bit disarming as we enter the music education culture.

That all being said, Ms. Robertson is very wise; she was insightful in keeping a running log of her daily challenges as she traversed the requisite pathway every new teacher must endure. We are the benefactors of her year-in-review as she prescribes the various solutions to the problems she faced. While many of the situations are specific for young teachers, most of the described circumstances are a close cousin to every rehearsal hall and music classroom; in other words, we can all learn from her portrayal of her year-one thoughts and feelings.

Kate's quick maturation is a result of her willingness to put herself in the driver's seat of responsibility. The welfare of the music program and the care-and-feeding of her young musicians serve as the center of her philosophical goals. She truly is a positive role model for every teacher.

Her "moment-of-truth" (in my opinion) is evident in her December writings when she embraces her ongoing frustrations by taking an honest look at her students and what motivates them to be involved in the music program.

She writes in her state of angst:

"It is like giving a gift and having it thrown back in your face. It is like preparing a fine feast only to have your family tell you they are not hungry. When students act as though they don't want to learn what you have to teach them, it is difficult not to take their attitude as a hurtful rejection, even though they probably don't realize their actions are creating that effect. As musicians, we are passionate about our art form and want everyone else to be also...sometimes that is just not the case.

One would think that students, especially high school age, are in music classes because they really want to be...because they feel that sense of enthusiasm about music that you do. Unfortunately, that is not always the story.

So how do you deal with students....? First of all, as much as you may want to...you cannot ever give up...."

Ah, there it is; **you can never give up.** It is the mantra of every successful teacher, or successful anyone, for that matter. As Winston Churchill said, "We must give up giving up."

As you consume the following pages, you will laugh, you may cry, and you will nod in agreement as you remember a similar situation in your own career. But most of all you will marvel at the exemplary commitment, dedication, and genuine love that is generated by this first year teacher, Catherine Bell Robertson.

Confessions of a First-Year Maestro will delight you as it stirs your soul and warms your heart.

...let the music begin....

acknowledgements

This book would not have been possible without the love, support, and contributions of the following people:

Thank you to:

My husband Cal and our dog "Jake" for being my biggest fans. I am the luckiest person in the world! I love you!

My mom and dad, Margaret and George, sister Amy, and Grandma Germaine for teaching me that anything is possible with hard work, and for your constant enthusiasm, belief, and encouragement. I love you!

My students...past, present, and future for allowing me to be your teacher. I hope you learn as much from me as I do from you. I'm glad and honored to be able to share in your lives.

All my teachers, past, present, and future, especially: Mr. Rapp, my high school band director, for being a wonderful role model; Mr. Hoefer, my college music education professor, who "made" me keep my first teaching journal during my student teaching experience; Mrs. Pickett, my high school English teacher, who always went above and beyond to encourage my writing; Dr. Hindson, my college private lesson instructor, for being a wealth of knowledge as well as a friend; and Dr. Conturno, my first "professional" mentor. You all have touched the future.

My friends and colleagues for sharing your knowledge and helping me "learn the ropes" along the way.

The staff at GIA Publications, Inc., especially Alec and Denise, for believing in my idea and being so wonderful to work with. I would also like to thank Yolanda Durán for her marvelous illustration and design.

You! Thank you for taking time in your busy schedule to read this book. I hope you will find it a noble companion to your own journey of teaching.

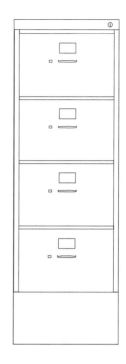

Confessions of a
First-Year Maestro

*An informative, quirky, and touching guide to
(almost) everything that will happen during your first
year of teaching music.*

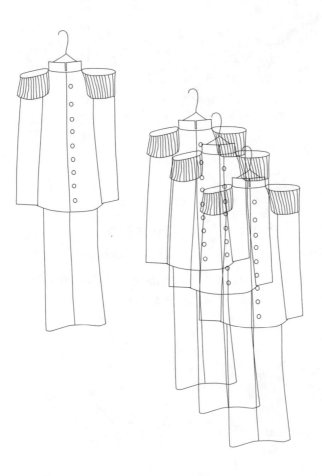

introduction

May 30, 2001

"Okay, this is our last performance of the year, let's make it a great one," I said to the Concert Band and Show Choir as we warmed up for the performance at our high school graduation ceremony. We performed "Pomp and Circumstance," the National Anthem and a recessional march. Although wonderful for parents and graduating Seniors, many people may think it was just another performance for me and the ensembles; that it all was pretty standard and typical.

But was it? Not to me. As I reflect on my first year of teaching, I know that seemingly typical ordinary experiences have really been extraordinary. As I led concerts, other performances, and rehearsals, as well as ran a music department for the first time, I knew that these were very special moments in my teaching career; my time as a first year teacher.

I teach at a private suburban high school in Wisconsin with a population of about 1,000 students, which in itself sounds pretty normal. The abnormal part is that for my entire first year, I was the only music teacher in the school. Not the only instrumental or vocal music teacher; I was the only music teacher for 1,000 students. My responsibilities included concert band, marching band, pep band, jazz band, string ensemble, a chamber music ensemble, chorus, concert choir, show choir, and a music appreciation class, as well as various study hall supervisions and smaller sectional rehearsals.

Now, before you call me crazy for taking on all of these responsibilities, allow me to give you some background knowledge. First of all, the situation would change my second year. The need for separate specialized teachers for both vocal and instrumental music was recognized by the administration and if I could "hang with them" for this first year, next school year, I would have help. Secondly, the school was in the area of the state where I really wanted to live. As the first of many pieces of advice in this book, don't ever let anyone tell you that your feelings on this subject should not matter in getting your first job. Your personal happiness outside of your workday often depends upon where you live, and is just as important as your job satisfaction. Thirdly, I came from a private, religious high school, and going back to that close-knit, family-based atmosphere appealed to me. So, I interviewed for the position in late June of 2000 and was called by the principal on the Fourth of July and offered the job. So I took it…maybe I still do need to be called crazy….

The notes and journal entries upon which this book is based were written at many different times: before and after school, between classes when a quick thought came to me, or at home. However, the majority of my thoughts were written in the study halls I supervised: between lesson plans, attendance taking, and the curbing of card games. I reflected back on the day or the week and wrote things that went well, things that I could improve on in the future, and things that I learned and felt. Even if you are not an eloquent writer or don't plan on writing a book, I highly suggest keeping a journal solely for your teaching experiences. Not only is it a therapeutic, healthy way of revealing your feelings, but it may also help you analyze your teaching, personal inter-actions, and planning. This ultimately made me a better teacher.

Although everyone's first year of teaching is different, my hope is that this book will give you a kindred spirit; an affirmation that someone else knows your struggles, hopes, and joys as a music educator. Whether you are a college student in a teacher-training program, a student teacher, a first-year teacher, or a veteran teacher, you will enjoy this journey through my first year in the field of education. Maybe all this book will do for you is raise questions; however, questions are good because they challenge you to look into yourself. Perhaps you will see yourself in many of my experiences. Maybe you can take some-thing away from the lessons I learned. At the least, I hope that my story will make you laugh, cry, scream in anger, sigh with contentment, and ultimately realize what a truly amazing profession music education is. Enjoy!

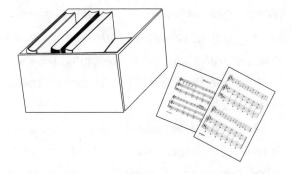

the basics

Interviewing for a teaching position—things your college career placement office might not have told you….

The process of interviewing for a teaching position, especially your very first job after college graduation, can be quite an intimidating experience. I felt the whole spectrum of emotions when I went through the interview process, from excited and confident to downright scared and even nauseous. All of these feelings are normal. The most important things to remember are to be positive, motivated, and very organized. Use simple aids like keeping lists for yourself. And always give yourself some free time each day as a stress release during the days, weeks, or months in which you are interviewing: go on a walk! Give yourself a break.

Let us assume that you have sent out your resume and/or various application packets to the schools in which you are interested. Give your materials a few days to arrive at the school, then call to confirm that your materials were received. Ask to speak directly with a principal or administrator after you speak with an office assistant. This is very important. When you speak with this administrator, keep things very brief, professional, and to the point. Introduce yourself, state that you are very interested in the open position, and that the district has received your application packet. Continue by saying that you are anxious for them to review your application and you look forward to the opportunity for an interview.

The administrator will probably not have much time to have a conversation with you, so you may think that this tactic will be fruitless. However, I guarantee that you will have impressed this administrator with your professionalism and persistence. This is a crucial contact, because the administrator will remember your name when he or she looks through the piles and piles of applicants. This persistence and self-motivation will help you stand out, which is exactly what you need to get that first interview.

Your next step toward success is the assembly of a portfolio. Portfolios seem to be a big buzzword in the education field lately, but creating one of your own should be fairly easy and fun. Portfolios are really nothing more than organized scrapbooks containing pieces that will help you look good during interviews. For someone right out of college, things to include in your portfolio would be projects, papers, evidence of volunteer participation, certificates of achievement, educational seminars, work-study experiences, student teaching information; use your imagination! In my portfolio, in addition to most of the above materials, I also have programs and posters from concerts I performed in, audio and video tapes, pictures from my college marching band, as well as pictures of me working with kids at a summer music camp (a side note: my current principal said that this evidence of my counseling and teaching at summer camps really impressed her in my interview, and frankly was a key factor in being offered my current position). Obviously, if you are already in the field of education, you will have many other ideas for the contents of your own personalized portfolio.

Make sure that your portfolio is presentable and well organized. Random pictures falling out of a binder and frayed edges won't get you any bonus points. Then, don't be shy! Bring your portfolio to your interview and take the initiative to show yourself off through this tool. Don't wait for the interview committee to ask! This was a mistake that I made in some of my early interviews: my snazzy portfolio never made it out of my briefcase. Along with being very nervous, I kept waiting for someone to ask, "Do you have anything to show us?" They wouldn't ask, so I wouldn't want to be pushy. Take a more assertive approach. For example, use your portfolio to tie in to an answer that you give: "Why, yes, I have worked with children with special needs. I got this certificate when..." You get the idea. Pretty soon after that, you will be paging through your portfolio with the interview team and describing all the wonderful things about you!

Okay, so the school district called and you have an appointment for the big interview. This deserves congratulations in itself. The powers that be liked your resume and have separated you from the masses of other applicants. Now, how do you continue to set yourself apart?

Whether you want to think about it or not, sometimes administrators see hiring a first year teacher as "a gamble." In two different interviews I had for my first job, the committee narrowed the candidates to me and one other person with prior teaching experience, and both times, they hired that other person. This is not meant to discourage you, but to emphasize not only the fact that you must set yourself apart from the crowd, but also that you are confident, well-trained, and ready for action!

In my mind, how to do this successfully is the same thing that you would tell your music students: practice, practice, and more practice! Practice answering sample interview questions; yes, aloud. If you can recruit a close friend or a family member to help you, that is even better. Listen to the tone of your voice, not merely the words you say. Practice eye contact. As silly as it sounds, use a mirror and have a professional conversation with yourself. Be assured of your walk, your handshake, and your posture. Everything you say or do sends a message.

This leads me right into advice about your attire. In the highly professional situation of an interview, there are really no exceptions. Men: a suit and tie, shined shoes, clean cut and shaven. Women: a dress, skirt and blouse or a pantsuit, all with appropriate shoes and accessories. Again, think purely on the basis of first impressions. Go back to your mirror and really look: if you were on an interview committee, would you hire you?

So, it's finally interview time. Hopefully you have arrived early. Think positive, relaxing thoughts as you wait in the office to meet your interviewers. A little nervousness is good, as it gives you energy and shows that you care about the outcome of the interview. Focus that energy into enthusiasm. You must convey your love of kids, of music, of education, not only in your words, but also in your face, your eyes, and your heart. Highlight things that make you a special asset to their school; like in my situation, where I attended a private religious high school like the school at which I interviewed. Someone who understood their mentality already and believed in their philosophies was very appealing. Find something unique to you that will help make the school a better place.

Now that the interview is over, you may encounter the toughest part of all; not the rejection, but the waiting. It is tough, but try your best to be patient when you are waiting to hear about the status of a position. I found it very frustrating, even consuming, waiting for the phone to ring. Take care of your mental and physical health and get your mind on other things, like you should during this entire process. It's even more critical now; go for that bike ride, go shopping, or spend time with a good friend. Before you do though, always send out a thank you card to the school district for the opportunity to interview. Address it to the main interviewer and hand-write it. Make it as personal and unique as possible. I suggest doing this the same day or the morning right after the interview.

Getting experience doing interviews is invaluable; do as many as you can. Situations deviate greatly among various school districts. I have interviewed with as few as one other person and as many as eight, with people ranging from administrators and other teachers to parents and students. Even if you don't think that you would be interested in a certain open position, do an interview for the experience of getting more comfortable with the whole process. Then, once that "dream job" comes along, you will be all the more prepared to give a great interview.

How many resumes should you send out? How many interviews will you obtain from sending out those resumes? You may hear all kinds of statistics about what percentage of your resumes and applications will result in a call for an interview. However, don't base your entire mindset on this. Obviously, everyone and every situation is different. But some general guidelines are as follows: if you only send out three resumes, don't get too upset if you don't receive any responses. Conversely, if you send out 30 and don't receive a phone call from even one school district, review your resume and application strategies. As a frame of reference, I sent out about 20 resumes over a period of about two months. I was called by eight of those schools to conduct an interview.

If you haven't been offered an interview or a position

yet, hang in there. There are plenty of places to look for job openings: newspapers, the Internet, college placement offices, and job fairs to name a few. In the world of music education, a great place to check for jobs is at a local music store. These people often service all the schools in a wide area and know who's leaving, retiring, going back to school, etc. before anyone else does. Keep trying and stay upbeat! "Your" job is out there....

the basics

*After accepting a position...did **my** music teacher ever have to do this stuff?*

So, you got the job. Congratulations! Go out and celebrate!

However, don't forget that your responsibilities start a long time before the first day of school. There are many things that you, as the new band director, choir director, orchestra director, or general music teacher should do as soon as you can before school starts into order to help your first year get off on the right foot.

The best way to create a great first impression as the new teacher in the building is pretty easy: show up! As soon as you are able after the deal is sealed, get into the school and put some time in getting used to the building, your classroom, and your office if you have one. Bring in some of your own personal items that you will use for teaching: books, music, etc. Set up some personal items that you will enjoy looking at every day that will help to make the place your own; hang pictures or posters on the walls, put that beloved trinket on your desk. Not only will these simple things make you feel more comfortable, but they will also give that feeling of comfort and belonging to others. When I first walked into my new music department, I found it very difficult to start inhabiting a space where someone else taught a mere six weeks before. It is very important to create an atmosphere of personalized renewal and energy for yourself and your students. The fine points of how you do that will be as individual as you are.

Maybe you will be lucky and come into a department that is well organized, clean, and easy to understand. Maybe you will have other members of the music department take you under their wing and walk you through "the basics." This is surely my hope for you…however, as I know first hand, this is not always the case….

A few days after I signed my contract, I came to my new school eager to work, to organize things the way I wanted them, and to make the department my own. The principal showed me the way down to the music department again, as she did during my interview. She admitted that she did not know the state of many things in the music department, but to go ahead with whatever organizational changes I felt necessary.

As she left me to my work, I realized what a huge task I had before me. There were file cabinets all over the room with stray pieces of music in them. There were folders with random jazz band pieces in them, none organized or stored together with a score. The pep band music was a disaster; anyone who's ever seen a cabinet full of little squares of music with no rhyme or reason knows that it's enough to drive you crazy! And the music office….I don't know how, or if, anything could have been kept straight in there. There was old junk mail, letters, papers, and clutter that was never thrown away. Cardboard boxes, empty opened envelopes, and plastic wrappings sat on the floor or were stuffed in desk drawers, just waiting to cause the next teacher grief and heartache. This is definitely something your professors don't prepare you for in your university methods classes. I felt overwhelmed and defeated before I even began.

But only for a little while. What you have to do in these situations is just pick a place to start and get to it. I began with the music office, now *my* office. I figured if I could make my office a safe haven first, it would give me a base from which to strike out at my other opponents. I dug into the mass of clutter, throwing away three monster-sized garbage bags of junk mail and old useless paperwork in a matter of about two hours. I moved file cabinets, situated the computer, emptied and restocked desk drawers, and did a lot of cleaning. I hung pictures and set up other things special to me. Once I got into the entire organization process, it was not that bad. Actually, it gave me great satisfaction to make the office mine and bring order to chaos.

Once I had the music office in good shape, I tackled some of the other looming projects. A piece of advice I have for you if you ever find yourself in a similar position is to get student help. Talk to other teachers or your principal and find out who the student leaders are in the music program. Give them a call, introduce yourself, tell them of your plans, and ask if they are available to help. Most of your best kids should jump at the chance to be one of the first to meet the new music teacher, as well as delight at the appeal of a leadership opportunity. It was great to have the help as well as the company as we sorted through the stacks of music, made piles on the floor that overtook the entire music room, and put them in order for perhaps the first time. Not only did things get organized, but I also met my first students and was able to bond with them (I think they enjoyed the pizza I bought them, too). Meeting students and getting to know them before school started was wonderful. It was comforting to have some familiar faces during those first couple days of the school year.

It may not sound like a very complex job, but the above cleaning process literally took about three weeks to completely finish. This is why you, as a new teacher, must check on the status of the department before the school year starts. Imagine trying to do all of those organizational things while you are teaching in the midst of September....

Even if your department is ship-shape when you are hired, you still have plenty of things to accomplish. Get class rosters and see what kind of numbers you are dealing with for all of your classes or performing groups. Go through the music library and see what the status is. Do you have twenty scores to chose from or two hundred? Start choosing various levels of pieces to try with your groups at the beginning of the year. Make sure there are enough copies for every instrument or voice. Design introductory lesson plans for each piece and think about your ideas for instructing the ensembles. Consider goals for the year, for yourself and for your classes to work toward.

In my case, there was a lot of administrative stuff for me to do as well. No concerts for the coming year were scheduled and since the school held the performances at a nearby college auditorium, finding open dates this close to the beginning of the school year was quite a process. Once the concert dates were finalized, I typed up date sheets for each performing group, stating these obligations. I also created a handbook, a document of about four pages that gave my rules and expectations for the music department (see sample in the reference section). Both the handbook and the date sheet were distributed to the students the first day of school. This is something I highly suggest you do, as it shows your students as well as your administration your control, organization, and forward thinking right from the start. Imagine standing in front of your chorus, for example, on the first day of school and having a student ask, "When is the fall concert?" and you having no idea....

My number one piece of advice is to be prepared. Put in the time before the school year starts in order to be very organized and ready for the beginning of the year. Nothing creates havoc in a classroom faster than a teacher who has no idea what is going on. Know what you want, have a plan for it, and communicate it clearly and confidently from the very first day.

Take a deep breath. I think we are ready to proceed into the depths of the journey....

August

As I explained in the previous chapter, I did a lot of planning and organization during the summer before my first year of teaching. This included much of my time in August. In more ways than just the weather, the heat definitely started to rise. Not only was I deeply involved with planning a curriculum for all of my classes which began August 29, but I also had another event to structure, one that was coming up much more quickly: marching band camp.

Now, I love marching band, but the logistics of the situation had me petrified. The only thing organized for the camp was that the week was set on the school calendar and the students were aware of it. So, I got to work.

Many of the tasks and ideas I used to prepare for this would be sound advice for any type of summer music camp. First of all, I ordered music, and in this case, a field show. We would not have gotten very far without that. The company I worked with was awesome. They understood my situation, rush delivered what I needed, and in general made my life much easier. When the materials arrived at school, students again helped to make sure there were enough copies to distribute to everyone for the first day. Next, I wrote an introductory letter to all the students and enclosed with it a schedule and explanation of the week of camp. This helps alleviate a lot of tension because it gives the students an idea of what to expect. In addition, I met with some of the upperclassmen and section leaders before camp started. This helped me discover what they already knew and in which direction to take them.

I also met with some people within the school to get a handle on administrative things. The athletic director gave me the home football game schedule. I checked with the maintenance person to request that lines be painted on the field for practice. I got to know all the various secretaries and budget people very quickly and very well. They informed me about all those essential concepts I needed to help the camp, and ultimately the music department run smoothly. I never thought about it before, but everything from learning about your department budget to where your mailbox is and how to use the phone system takes time. All of this, combined with my own personal prep time and occasionally getting out of school to enjoy the final days of summer, kept me pretty busy.

All of a sudden, it was the Monday morning of marching band camp. I was excited and very nervous. But I figured I prepared as well as I knew how, so everything should go well. And it did. The kids worked hard on marching and learning the drill and music. The section leaders, drum major, and alumni who came back to help were also very dedicated. The weather was beautiful… what more could you want for your first marching band camp?

If you can, do your own summer music camp. It may be difficult to schedule your first year, especially if it is not already planned and something the kids and parents expect considering summer vacations, etc. But the benefits are outstanding. During this first camp, we learned about 75% of the drill, which saved a lot of time and effort once the school year started. Think about the concepts that you could get a head start on with your ensembles! But even more importantly, a summer music program creates friendships, teamwork, a common goal, and "esprit de corps" if you will, before the school year begins. Your students are excited and dedicated toward that common goal before they are bombarded with all the other stress that school and extra-curricular activities often impose.

For me, the camp was a great experience. Not only was it very successful in the areas I hoped and expected—learning the music and drill, bonding and working together, and refining marching skills—but it was also meaningful in ways I didn't expect. For the first time, I felt in charge of something substantial that was a success. Throughout college and student teaching, there is always someone there to guide you along. But this camp was something I could really assume pride and ownership of as being my accomplishment. My work paid off. My training proved valuable. My hopes and dreams of being a music director were realized. The feeling was incredible! My first undertaking at my first job was a success.

In-services

The week after marching band camp were in-service meetings for the staff at my new school. I know what you're thinking; groan, meetings! Don't go in with the assumption that in-services are boring. Maybe I was just excited about everything dealing with my first teaching position, but I thought these meetings were great. In fact, there are concepts used here that would be useful in any meeting situation.

August 24

Today was my first in-service at my new school. Feels kinda weird because for so many teachers, this is their first time in the building since June, and then there's me. A new teacher, but one who has been working since early July. The principal introduced all the new teachers, so that was nice. However, I felt like everyone knows me and I don't know anyone. There is a faculty of about 70 teachers, and for me that is pretty intimidating, because I will never learn all of their names. Maybe there could've been an ice-breaker or name game played?

Anyway, I thought that in-services would be really lame. But I was wrong—at least the ones here are pretty interesting and involving. We had an inspirational speaker and we acted out ideas instead of just sitting and listening. A good model for the classroom.... Being we are a religious school, we also had a prayer service and a Mass. I thought that it was a very bonding experience.

> I know that the public schools can't do it,
> but perhaps they could do something with an
> inspirational painting, poem, or piece of
> music to help focus and bond teachers
> together at the beginning of a new year.
> Even though I will not remember everyone's
> name right away, I'm glad that several
> teachers came up and introduced themselves
> to me. It made me feel welcome.

Ready...

The day before the "real" first day of school was freshmen orientation day, which I thought was a great idea.... I was a freshman, too! It was a nice way to ease into the concept of school starting. For the nervous ninth graders, it was a non-stressful way for them to find their way around the building. The day only lasted until noon, which was great because it let me make the finishing touches for the big first day of school. It also allowed me the time to do all kinds of other things that you will find are necessary when you begin a new job; filling out paperwork for insurance, paychecks, benefits, retirement plans, etc. All of these extraneous things you have to do for any new job can be time-consuming and over-whelming, but don't let it get the best of you. Make friends with your business manager at school and don't be afraid to ask all the questions you need to settle your affairs. My advice is to get it done as soon as possible, so you don't have to worry about it once the school year really gets underway.

Set...

My school is on an A day/B day rotating schedule, which means the teachers and students have the same schedule every other day. All of the "core" subjects like math, English and science meet every day. However, all of the music classes and some other elective classes meet every other day. On A days, I taught chorus, string ensemble, concert band (marching band), show choir, and sectional lessons, and I supervised a study hall. On B days, chamber music ensemble, concert choir, jazz band and music fundamentals met, and I supervised another study hall. (For a sample schedule, please see the reference section).

Teach!

August 29 – The first day of school

My first class on my first day was Chorus, the biggest choir in the school, with an enrollment of about 50 kids from all four grade levels. Sitting in front of them, watching them talk, congregate, and laugh, I had a

fleeting moment of sheer panic. For an instant,
I was so nervous, my mind went blank and I
wasn't sure what to do next. But in the blink
of an eye, it was gone and I was ready to
go...I guess my nerves were just testing me.

Most of my first day went pretty smoothly.
Mainly I distributed the music department
handbook, talked about concert dates, and
asked the students to introduce themselves.
They seemed very friendly, accepting, and energetic.

The hard part of the day was Marching
Band. Having not seen them for 10 days since
the band camp, their memories were poor.
We did so well during the week of camp and
today it looked like we barely accomplished
anything. Slow, sloppy action and poor attitudes.
Hopefully it is all the excitement because of
the first day of school that has them distracted. Camp was so successful merely a week
and a half ago...I know that that knowledge
is still with them.

On the first day of school, some of the students
started making fun of their last band director. I
simply told them to change the subject. It may seem
innocent, but there is a danger of a serious trap.
Make sure you don't join in on any bashing or even
ask about what the previous director did that was
so bad. Not only would partaking in the conversation be unprofessional and inappropriate, but it
would diminish your credibility and might make you
seem insecure.

August 30

My first B day. I had different classes
and met some more great kids. I introduced
the handbook and concert dates and organized
for the year with these groups as well. I
felt that it had to be done right or the kids
would be confused. As a first year teacher,
I really wanted to be efficient and taken
seriously. The kids introduced themselves to
their classmates and me. I also gave the
Concert Choir and Jazz Band some choices
about music. Before school started, I picked
out several pieces that I thought would be
worthwhile and let them vote on which they
would prefer. I think they liked this idea; I
like it because it gives the students a role in
controlling their own ensemble.
I already know that one of my many challenges for the year will be my Fundamentals
of Music class. It is a new class, and I'm not
sure how it was "advertised" when students
registered for it, but I have many different
ability levels within the class. I have my
best flute player who is going to college for
music performance next year right alongside
sophomores who are not in another music
class and can't even read notes! How will I
gear the class to make it a beneficial experience for everyone?

I'll keep you posted on that....

Since the marching band's first performance was
coming up quickly on September 1st, I had a plan to

get us more rehearsal time. The school has four lunch periods. The students have a class over two of these, eat lunch for one and have a homeroom for one. Luckily, band is scheduled as a lunch period class. This means that everyone in band eats lunch at the same time. So, I got permission for all band members to be excused from their homeroom to give us an extra 25 minutes of rehearsal. The first of many stunts by the new music teacher....

Seriously: be motivated! Be creative! Try new things like this! However, don't throw caution to the wind; always be prepared and organized...read on.

August 31

Back to an A day again—started chair placements with String Ensemble, beginning music and warm-ups with choirs. Some fabulous voices, especially in the Show Choir. Outside rehearsal for Marching Band with the Color Guard today. I got extra time from the lunch periods to rehearse, so that worked really well. I tried to be very organized and sent memos to the affected teachers of the kids who would miss their homeroom for the rehearsal. Most of the kids did a much better job than just two days ago, although it was very hot outside. Some had bad attitudes and didn't want to work hard. It was a difficult balance for me. I wanted to encourage them and tell them they looked good. But I also wanted to really lay into them and tell them to shape up and work harder. I'm not sure about the right balance to use....

So far, things were off to a good start. But these final thoughts from my journal during the month of August were concepts I struggled with all year. How to motivate without frustration, how to praise without coddling? It seems as though questions and discoveries are just beginning.

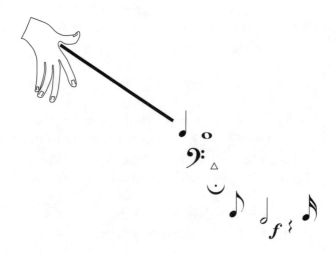

September

September…the month-long moment of truth. Organizing, planning, and the reciting of rules are all very necessary, but now the teaching really begins. Problems arise that you never planned for. Some students start to show their "true colors," to put it nicely. But take heart, because some truly incredible and amazing things happen, too… like our first marching band performance….

September 1

The Marching Band arrived early to the home field for warm-up and rehearsal before the big first game. It took a long time to get everyone going, but we had a good run-through once they were organized. We were to perform a simple pre-game—marching out onto the field from an end zone in a block formation to play the National Anthem and the fight song. At half time, we were going to perform three of the four pieces in our drill.

Pre-game was upon us. As I was standing on the podium watching them march down the field, all in step and looking sharp, I thought, "I helped them do this!" I started to cry…I had to bite my lip to keep it from quivering!

Pre-game went well, and half time was great! We got a standing ovation from parents and my principal hugged me after the game! I know that there are still little things to fix, such as making sure everyone is wearing their white gloves, etc. But overall, things were great for our first performance of the year. It was an amazing experience... and I am very exhausted!

During the first full week of September, I really got into the groove of my schedule and the classes I taught. I started to learn the similarities and differences among all the groups. It was exciting to put plans and ideas into motion. Some things worked well and other ideas I had to modify, but the important thing was that I learned from all of them. In certain ways it was overwhelming, but I felt I was ready for the challenge of really diving into the school year.

September 5

Tuesday after a long Labor Day weekend. I congratulated the Band again for their great performance on Friday—I am excited to watch the video of the performance in a few days. Really getting into the teaching aspect of my classes—beyond organizational stuff—which is a good thing, because tomorrow the choirs have to perform at the first all-school Mass. As I learned with the Marching Band, it is tough to put a quality performance together at the beginning of the school year without conducting a camp or having many extra rehearsals. So I started the Chorus on familiar music that most of them already know from last year or their own churches.

Started various pieces of music with the String Ensemble and sat them according to their chair placements we did last week. The Band got a little break from rehearsal after my congratulations—we did the handbook, explained the sectional lesson schedule, and handed out some concert band music. They were a tough group to settle down; I think they are used to being outside and louder because of marching practices. Still, I am concerned that they cannot make that shift to indoor rehearsal behavior more quickly. The Chorus is a tough group also, mainly because of size. Good progress in the Show Choir—they know all of our music for the church performance tomorrow. We began work on other pieces. They were making some nice chords.

Have been using the study halls I supervise to write notes and lesson plans. My main concern at the moment is finding that effective balance between being nice and being firm with some groups, especially ones with bigger enrollment.

September 6

Choir performance at the all-school Mass today. It was almost more nerve-wracking for me than the Marching Band performance because this was in front of all the kids' peers and my teaching peers. They sang well though; it helped that we chose familiar music. Although I'm already noticing that some students don't open their mouths to sing—they kinda mumble. Which actually gives me a great idea...I will do individual and/or small group music checks with the choirs. I will be able to see if they know the music, plus it will help me to learn names better. So far, that is a big struggle for me. Since I have so many students, I have a difficult time remembering names. I think that seeing the kids more one-on-one or in smaller groups will help.

Played a team game in Fundamentals today and worked on some basic music theory worksheets together. I like talking with this group and having discussions about concepts to check their knowledge more than giving them quizzes.

The number one way to help curb discipline problems and get kids "on your side" is to learn their names as quickly as possible. If students know you don't know their names, they are more likely to cause trouble. Not only that, but how valued will they feel if you don't know who they are?

If you're like me, you have a horrible time learning and remembering names. Try as many tactics as you can. Meet with your students individually or in small groups for lessons or other certain assignments:

seeing students in that manner helped me more than seeing them in a larger group. Ask the yearbook staff if there are old yearbooks you can borrow, then look at the kids' photos and try to match their name with their face. Find more ideas to use from your fellow teachers. Not only could this help your memory, but this also may be a great topic to help start a conversation with your new colleagues or a way to get to know them better.

> **September 7**
>
> I had some cool things planned today, so I was excited. In Chorus, we started an arrangement of "The Water is Wide." We worked on it part by part and the group really liked how it sounded when we put it back together. The whole process of rehearsing with them today was neat. We listened to some CD recordings during String Ensemble of pieces we are working on. I had them follow along in their own music during the recording. They enjoyed it and were especially impressed by "In the Hall of the Mountain King" because of its tempo. Band was mediocre—still lots of talking whenever we're not playing. We rehearsed inside and started concert band music today. I'm trying to alternate between concert and marching rehearsals so they don't get too used to playing with a "field" tone. It also gives them some variety—keeps them on

> their toes. The students in Show Choir want
> to do a musical revue, so I am in the process
> of ordering some music on approval for that.
> Good showing of student leadership in this group.
>   Today my voice hurt from all the talk-
> ing/singing/yelling. I hope that I am not
> doing any permanent damage—sure that I'm
> just not used to using my voice this much.

The voice thing may happen to you also. It was scary for me… great, here I am, my first month of school getting laryngitis; or worse, damaging my vocal chords for life, I thought. But it was nothing, your voice gets used to the extra activity. Drink lots of water and try not to strain your voice by talking loudly or yelling all the time…of course, the "not yelling" option might not work for some….

> September 8
>
>   Interesting the things that you don't know
> as a first-year teacher. Either I missed the
> memo or just plain forgot, but today was
> picture day. I guess it is always the first
> Friday in September. Well, I looked okay,
> but not exactly how I would've planned if I
> knew it was picture day. I hope that I don't
> end up with a picture that everyone will draw
> devil ears on or something in the yearbook….

Anyway, today I gave the Chamber Music Ensemble students some time to practice their parts independently, which gave me the opportunity to visit each one of them and check their progress. I was a little disappointed because they all needed a little bit of a jump-start; in the larger ensembles, they are leader types. Weird. Concert Choir got into their concert music for the year after spending classes so far prepping for the Mass performance. They were quick learners—amazing difference between them and the Chorus; between students serious about music and those doing it maybe just because their friends are. Today was our first really productive Jazz rehearsal. They are starting to listen to me and each other better, plus I handed out some easier charts. I think I began the year with music that was way too difficult, so that probably didn't help their attention spans these past few days, either. I should have had a wider variety of music for them right from the start.

Don't let your first week of "real" teaching overwhelm you. You have a lot of responsibilities, from taking attendance and learning names to passing out music and assigning lockers, school instruments and folders, and not to mention the management of a classroom full of "creative" children. Hopefully somewhere in there, some teaching and learning take place, too. If you think that your first week of teaching is basic survival and keeping your head above water, you're right. And that's okay. Don't despair if you were not a candidate for Teacher of the Year during your first week. I know I wasn't. Don't think that you were a failure because students didn't have enormous musical epiphanies during the first lessons you taught. I know my students didn't. You are still a learner also. Quality and progress take time.

September 11

As I write this entry in study hall, it never ceases to amaze me how different kids are—some sitting and working quietly and some talking the entire time.

Anyway, the Chorus is still a challenge for me with so many kids in there and having to do a lot of rehearsing with the smaller sections within the group. I have to figure out ways to keep them more engaged. The String Ensemble is the exact opposite—you can hear a pin drop when I talk to them. Sometimes, I actually get nervous because I hope I'm saying intelligent things that will hold this great attention! In Band, we watched the video of last week's game performance. I think it is great for them to see themselves from an outside perspective. We also started some new concert band music. I instructed them to clap a difficult rhythm and got some eye rolls, like clapping was

---

"baby stuff" for them. However, their minds changed pretty quickly when they realized how much it aided them in learning the music. In Show Choir, we had a heated discussion about which musical revue to do this fall. I finally had to calm the students down and make them participate in an anonymous vote, with the final decision being mine. Two seniors asked to be "student directors" for the production, so that was cool. So far, they are doing so well on their other pieces. It is rewarding as a music educator to be so picky with them and talk about such advanced musical concepts when they are just starting a piece.

Oh, you'll *love* this next story. My only advice to prevent this from happening to you is to be very aware of your room and your surroundings. The music rehearsal room is a large room, with percussion closets and storage lockers on one side and my office, the music library, and practice rooms on the other. It is very difficult to watch everyone, everywhere, all the time, especially if I am doing work in my office. But that is probably not a viable excuse for what happened....

September 12

Pot smoking day.... For someone from a small town with a religious background, this one really threw me for a loop. A few students came to me in my office and ratted out another student, not even one involved in any music classes, who had smoked pot in one of the percussion closets while I was in my office. Boy, did I feel stupid. The principal and company came down to investigate and "smell" the place, but we did not catch the individial red-handed. As it is hard to punish a kid upon what other kids say, the administration simply let this person know they will be watching so there will not be a next time.

I, of course, felt like the biggest dummy on the planet. Even though the principal and others said that it was not my fault and not to be hard on myself, I felt totally responsible for letting something like that occur in my room—an atmosphere that I cherish and want to be a safe place for my students. I guess in a way it was good that it happened, because now I will be a lot more aware of who is around and what they are doing.

September 14

Today is Thursday and the last day of the week for the students because the faculty is going on a retreat tomorrow. Good Jazz Band rehearsal—for some reason, it seems to be an every other rehearsal with them— one good, the next one yuck. Worked on articulations and it seemed to help them sight-read and play better in general. Some of my String Ensemble students came into Fundamentals today to give a string instrument demonstration, as we are going through the different families of instruments. They were acting like they were listening, but when I led a discussion afterwards, their retention was pretty low. Assigned an essay a few days ago to be handed in today. Only six of ten students handed something in and only two were done decently. I am trying to treat them like young adults and want them to learn responsibility, but I don't know if they can handle it. I want the class to be enjoyable, but I want them to take it seriously also; again I have to find that balance.

As I read over this particular journal entry, now older and wiser, I wanted to scream the phrase, "Define your expectations!" It is something that I did with my performing ensembles, but I don't think that I did it very well with this "classroom" class. Of course I gave them a syllabus stating the goals of class, what we would be covering, and what kind of assignments they could expect. But what I did not do very well was explain *how* they would be graded on those things. And I really didn't realize that I screwed up on this aspect until the summer after this first year of teaching when I went to a seminar on assessment. I didn't make my expectations clear—I didn't set them up to succeed.

Let's face it, some students will never need to be told how to do things or how to strive toward a high ability level. They always work hard, they always do quality work, they always go for the "A." But I forgot that not all students are like that.

Students in your classes need to know right from the start what your expectations are. Don't assume they know that they have to turn essays in on time or that when they write that essay for your Fundamental of Music class that you expect correct grammar, punctuation, and spelling, just as if they were composing it for English class. I have to admit that these things sounded like common sense; at least that was how I felt the entire school year. But as you continue with me along the journey of the school year, you will hear more stories of woe in the department of Fundamentals of Music.

Granted, I did not have some of the best students enrolled in this class. In fact, I think about half of them took the class because they thought it was going to be a "blow off" class. But that is not the point. As much as they might not have tried, *I* also failed *them* in not providing more guidance as to what quality work meant to me.

I mention this early in the year not because I knew it then, because I obviously did not, but to give you a little help in doing a better job than I did in this area. In the reference section, there are examples of *rubrics* that I designed the summer after my first year of teaching, enlightened after an assessment seminar. Rubrics are guidelines that you can hand out at the beginning of the school year, with the assignment of a project, or for use as an aid for taking daily participation grades. I strongly encourage you to utilize them any time you see fit in order to define your expectations clearly. In a sense, this gives students a checklist to see what they need to do to achieve a certain level of performance, be it for a written assignment, presentation, class discussion, or artistic performance. There are no mysteries: "I don't know what the teacher is looking for on this assignment," and there can be no argument from parents: "Why did my child receive this grade?" There are entire education books solely on the use of rubrics, but I would be remiss if I did not at least touch on their importance. Clear expectations are essential for more effective teaching and learning.

September 15

Today was the off-campus faculty retreat and another football game tonight. I was enlightened at the retreat, but not necessarily by the topics or the presenter. In fact, the main speaker was really annoying, which in a way caused the enlightenment...let me explain. I was sitting in the second to the last row at the retreat. Little did I know that behind me were teachers who, once they decided

---

that the presenter was irritating, proceeded
to talk, laugh, and make jokes the entire
day. I was very disenchanted—this behavior
from teachers? Who want kids to listen and
pay attention whenever they are speaking?
Even though the retreat was doing nothing
for me, the speaker had an annoying voice
and laugh, and these people behind me were
blabbing, I did my best to be at least quiet
and respectful. I thought it was the least I
could do, since that is what I want when I
am speaking in front of a group. I thought
that the older you become, the more mature,
responsible, and respectful you grew. I guess
it is more dependent upon your character.

So then I had a horrible headache from
the retreat. It was 5 p.m. and the Band was
supposed to be at the field to begin rehearsal
and warm-up for the game. All of four kids
were there on time. I grew more and more
irate as the minutes went by: two weeks ago
went so well, why are they slacking now? I
felt embarrassed because my boyfriend was
there. I felt vulnerable in front of the band
members who were actually there on time. I
don't like feeling disorganized and not in
control, especially right before a performance.
Eventually, everyone arrived and the show
went fine. In fact, some aspects were better
than last time, but that does not excuse
problems with punctuality or attitude.

So, the rule for that week was to expect the
unexpected… unprofessional faculty members,

disobedient students, and fashionably late band members. My guess is that you also will run into things early in the school year that might try to diminish your faith and good humor. Don't let them. Keep trying new things, but be rock solid in your beliefs and ideals.

During this next week, I began to pull myself out of solely thinking about school and into more of how school was personally affecting *me*. Along with that, my confidence was building and relationships with my students were becoming more solidified. This doesn't mean that I felt like a master yet. But I always worked on it.

September 18

Recording day—listened to recordings in almost all of my classes today. Think that it's a great learning and reference tool. In order to motivate students in Chorus to use better diction, I brought in some recordings of popular artists like U2, Sting, etc., and asked them to bring some in as well. We played certain songs and talked about whether or not we could understand what they were singing and related it back to the use of good diction. It was a fun exercise. Also listened to examples of relevant pieces in Strings and Show Choir. I gave Band their deserved lecture concerning last Friday's lack of punctuality, responsibility, team effort, and good attitudes. I didn't want to be too

hard on them, but wanted them to know why
Friday was unacceptable. It seemed like they
listened well, so hopefully they will put it into
practice next time.

September 19

Today, I learned how something very small
can totally change one's mood and outlook on
everything. Toward the end of the day, I
had a few free minutes to stop in the library
and check my email. I received an unexpected
message from an old college "friend" that
was quite nasty. It really shook my focus
and I was very disturbed by it. But when I
made my way back to the music department
from the computer lab, a few of my students
said "Hi" and "How are you?" to me, and we
continued to make a little conversation. The
students probably didn't realize it, but they
really made my day. It was amazing how much
this seemingly small interaction really meant
to me. It didn't take all the hurt away from
the email incident, but it reminded me to be
more centered in life's everyday joys, not
the least of which being the smile of a teenager.

When you step outside your own problems and
let yourself be open to possibilities, amazing things
will happen. Think about how this can work for you,
both professionally and personally. And never

underestimate your potential to make or break someone's day. After this incident, I consciously tried to greet more students and faculty. It helped me...maybe I could help someone else.

September 20

Raining today, but took the Band outside to march anyway for part of the period. With everything coming up, such as Homecoming and community parades, we needed the practice. Little bit of whining, but I asked for their cooperation and told them they were tougher than the football players for doing this, so I think they liked that. We even got some productive work done.

"Success is not always fun and easy," I said.

What I am noticing this week is that I have been very tired and falling asleep on the couch by 9 p.m. I give away all my energy during the day. At night, when I want to do something for myself or with friends, I'm worn out. Part of me is upset about this.

September 21

I wonder if I have established a good balance between being "likable" and "understanding" of the students and maintaining discipline and structure. Sometimes I feel I'm too lax. Not necessarily during class, but concerning the subject of students and their

> free periods. I've let pretty much anyone come down to the music room during their lunch or homeroom. Sometimes they literally take over my office when I'm with a class in the music room. Part of me feels this is okay—kids need a place to go—I guess as long as they're not causing trouble or smoking like last time! But I also feel like I need a place that's only mine, even though I want to be as student-centered as possible. I just want to avoid anyone taking advantage of me.

Whoa, stop right there. This was another problem that plagued me all year and I should have stopped it before it even started. But that is one of hardest things about being a first-year teacher; breaking patterns that were set up before you arrived and making new rules, neither of which usually set you up to win a popularity contest.

Students told me at the beginning of the year that they were always allowed to come down to the music department during their open times to study, talk, or practice in one of the practice rooms or the music office. It seemed innocent enough, so I agreed. Pretty soon, however, the music department became the social hangout of the school, especially during periods when I had class in the music room and could not supervise them...how convenient.

At first, it made me feel good; wow, all these kids wanted to be in *my* room, what a compliment.

Try again. Most students will see how much they can take advantage of any new teacher. This doesn't mean they're bad kids, or even that they are doing it intentionally, but it does mean you have to be aware of it. In my situation, students took my good nature a little too far. They began eating their lunch in the music area (a big no-no), screaming and laughing outrageously while I was trying to teach a class in the next room, and leaving big messes of papers and other garbage on the floor when they eventually left. As the year went on, I got the issue more under control, but still had on and off battles with certain students and started giving out demerits. It was not a fun thing to do, and being a baby-sitter or the food police wasn't what I wanted to invest my time in.

Most music departments deal with this issue. Kids enjoy hanging out in the band room, choir room, or orchestra room. They feel a sense of belonging and safety (again, which is one reason why the pot incident upset me so much). To some degree, it is fine for kids to see the music department as a social place. In fact, it can be a great way for you as the teacher to get to know your kids better. But, if you find yourself in a situation that is getting out of control, don't be afraid to stand your ground or to make new rules. Get assistance from administration to back you up. Give students a compromise or alternative; for example, instead of the music room or practice rooms being taken over during the school day, I allowed kids to socialize there for a certain amount of time before and after school on most days. They were usually present at those times anyway, and I was more available to supervise their activities, my only distraction being work at my desk that I could easily do at the same time. My sincere advice on this subject is to not do anything you don't feel 100% comfortable with. Remember that your duties as a music educator should not suffer because students want to have a social hour.

Next year, my policies will be altogether different. If you are currently experiencing these problems, don't wait; make the changes now. It will help the rest of the school year continue much more smoothly. No one will be allowed in my office without me there. Period. No one will be allowed to do anything expect practice in a practice room; there are study halls and the library to do homework in. I will have to write the student a pass to come to the music department; they cannot just waltz in from anywhere. If students have my permission to be in the music department, they cannot be disruptive to whatever class is going on at the time. And if they blow it, I will deny them the privilege of using the music room during their open time. I will stress this as an issue of respect and responsibility, which I firmly believe are just as crucial to teach as any scholastic subject. Will this new policy be harsher than last year? Yes. Will it make kids upset? Maybe. Will it alienate kids and turn them off to the music department? I don't think so. Will it help make the music department a better place in the long run? Definitely.

September 22

First Friday of a full five day week. The principal came down to the music room today during Show Choir and we sang her a piece that we were working on. She loved it! She was very supportive and complimentary—that felt really good, hopefully for the kids as much as for me. The end of the day today was cool, too. Lots of kids came by my office and said "Bye" and "Have a nice weekend" as they picked up their instruments to take home, which in itself was great—they were not leaving them here over the weekend! One of my seniors interested in majoring in music let me know about his upcoming college visit and audition at the university I attended, so that made me feel good. Also got a supportive phone call from an area university band director welcoming me and asking if I needed anything. It was a very emotionally satisfying day.

September 25

I got a great idea for Fundamentals class today—the only way it could've been better was if I thought of it before class instead of after. Today we looked at scores to band, choir, string, and jazz pieces and pointed out

> the similarities and differences among them.
> They did a really nice job, so I got the idea
> to copy a page from each one and have them
> do a compare/contrast essay. I prepared it
> right after class to give them next time, but
> I wish that I would've been able to think
> ahead enough to have prepared it for home-
> work today.

This journal entry illustrates what knowledge-able teachers do really well and what young teachers sometimes falter on: preparing brainstorms and new ideas *effectively.* Often, the difference between a first-year teacher and a more experienced one is that element of forward thinking, as well as the wisdom of knowing exactly where and how to use ideas to best help the students learn. We are on our way....

> September 26
>
> Another busy A day. Not a very effective
> day with the Chorus. The other two choirs
> have good singers and strong leadership, but
> this choir has less confident singers—they
> seem to forget most of what we do from
> rehearsal to rehearsal. Plus they do not sing
> out, even when they do know the music. To
> add to the mix, my own inept piano playing
> skills irritate me as does my even more inept
> student piano accompanist who doesn't bring

his music to class. Music checks are going to be a necessity with this group. The Strings are improving their skills little by little each day. I am trying to encourage them to play with more passion, dynamics, and energy because they play very timidly. Sectional lessons for Band are going well. The band rehearsed outside in nice weather—finally—to continue preparations for the Homecoming game. The beautiful day made it easy to work hard; when the students concentrate, everything looks great.

September 27

I just do not like lecturing to my Fundamentals of Music class, mainly because I am not good at it. I don't know how other degree programs for teachers are, but at my university, there was not a class for future music teachers on how to give good lectures. I am used to directing a musical group, stopping them, making a few comments, and resuming to conduct. I can tell that the students are bored when I lecture and I am not used to looking at those dull lost faces. "Rehearsal faces" are usually much more engaged. It is difficult for me to devote time to preparing a lecture when I have 8 other classes to think about. Today, I gave them the essay from Monday, so that should be a good assignment for them. But I still feel like an incompetent bad teacher in that class.

Both Jazz Band and the Chamber group were also frustrating today because it doesn't sound like they are practicing their music individually. It is expected in these groups even more than other ensembles, as all of their pieces are "one on a part." Sometimes it sounds like they are reading the music for the first time when in reality they've had it for almost a month.

September 29 – Friday

Today was Homecoming—there was a half day of classes, then a pep rally and the Big Recess, where all the kids eat lunch together outside and a few garage bands play. Kinda cool idea. Classes were obviously pretty short, but Jazz Band had a great rehearsal. Because of the short classes, I picked a few spots to isolate in certain pieces and they ended up much improved.

I did not like the pep rally at all. First of all, it's tough to play in all the "correct" places where the pep rally team wants you to without rehearsing or talking about it beforehand. I received an outline in my mailbox of the pep rally events with little guidance or explanation. Plus the band kids seem to have a real pride problem. When we finally figured out where in the sequence of events we were supposed to play, the band didn't play very loud (like I know they can) and looked timid in front of the whole school. I will have to tell them that they have to have pride in themselves before anyone else will.

Our performance at the Homecoming game itself went well. We performed the whole show for the first time, plus the pom pom squad danced with us for one piece and a twirler performed during two pieces. Everyone was awesome: the band received lots of compliments and they seemed to be very pleased with themselves. I was a little disturbed because I personally accepted lots of compliments both on the pep rally and the marching show, when I thought that the Band's pep rally performance was pathetic. Do people know the difference? Are they just being nice? I have no idea. I felt really great after the Homecoming game, though. Punctuality was not an issue this week, so that was a plus. It all came together; the students worked well, had fun and were appreciated.

I hope it is apparent that by the end of my first month teaching, I learned many new things; things that college never taught me how to deal with. From pot-smoking music room invaders to fly-by-the-seat-of-your-pants pep rally planning, be open to that new knowledge. At this early point in the school year, make some notes for yourself. Remember things that worked well for you and jot them down; that's the easy part. It is a bit more difficult to walk down the dark sidewalks of your mistakes. But if you can learn something from those shortcomings and apply them to future situations, then you can grow both professionally and personally. Take something away from every single experience. And keep forging ahead… the year has just begun.

October

October, the month of contradictions and balancing acts. Over a month of school has gone by and yet you still feel like a rookie. Certain things start slowing down, while others are kicking into high gear. It becomes a strain to juggle paperwork with teaching, to balance entering grades into the computer and entering into friendly conversations with students. You spend hours and hours preparing for performances and other engagements, yet when they finally arrive, they fly by. However, one thing that remains constant is the amount you will learn as a new teacher during this month and all other months of the school year. The leaves on the trees may be falling as autumn arrives, but your knowledge, experiences, and perspectives will keep raising you to new heights.

October 2 - Monday

Today was the day after Homecoming weekend, so it was difficult for kids to focus. Had to tell a lot of them to put their pictures away, etc. The Chorus is slowly getting better—today I told them about their music checks coming up for the rest of the week, so hopefully those will go well. I know that some students don't know their music very well, so this should be a good way to find out who isn't practicing the way they should. Plus the music checks will be a good way to reinforce learning names, as I am so poor at it.

October 3

I took a sick day today. I stayed home and hated it. I kept worrying about what was happening at school. I guess I am a full-fledged teacher now....

October 4

Day after my sick day—I felt like I had a lot of catching up to do, although I know it really wasn't that much. Just felt out of the loop and behind—my control freak nature trying to take over. I had a talk with my principal, Dr. V., to ask about how things went yesterday and she was very complimentary; in fact, she had even taken two of my classes: Chamber Ensemble and Jazz Band. She said they both sounded great and had productive rehearsals. However, when I asked some of the jazz kids how they played, they admitted that they did not play well at all. I know that my principal knows some things

> about music, but did she really think they
> sounded good? Or was she just being nice? I
> know that the Jazz Band still needs a lot of
> work, so for me to hear "They sound great!"
> feels weird.
>
> Band looked good during their street march-
> ing today. Started Chorus music checks and
> they were going well—most students were
> singing louder and better in these small groups
> than they do in full rehearsal! I think that's
> goofy...I thought they would be more nerv-
> ous to sing in front of me in a smaller group
> versus in a large ensemble, but they sounded
> wonderful—now to get that into the full
> rehearsal setting....

False praise is far, far worse than criticism. More than likely, my principal really did think the Jazz Band sounded good. The teachers who told me the Pep Band sounded great at the Homecoming rally last week probably genuinely thought that. Which is fine...for them. But be very cautious about sharing these statements with your students or internalizing them yourself. *You* are the music director! If others comment that your ensemble sounds fantastic and you don't share that feeling, what joy do you receive from the performance? If you know that your students have not learned what you set out to teach them, what goal has been reached?

Shout genuine, warranted compliments about your students from the rooftops. But telling students about praise from other sources when you as the teacher do not think that it is deserved is very dangerous. It gives the students a phony impression of themselves and their abilities and eventually will result in lower standards. False praise from your lips is even worse. Musicians know when they are playing something well or badly. Even young children know this: they may not know *why* their performance sounded strange, but most times they know when they did not play something correctly. Therefore, these students are relying on you, their teacher, to help them strive toward improvement. If you say "Hey, that was great!" when it was far from great, you are not only letting that student down, but you are diminishing their faith in you as their trusted instructor.

But how do you keep their spirits up if you are constantly telling them the things they are doing wrong? Sometimes it is difficult to know exactly how to phrase constructive criticism to children in order to be most effective. What is most effective for me is to find at least one thing that the group or individual did well and comment on that first, then move on to the challenges. For example, if you are teaching a one-on-one music lesson and the student completely loses tempo, comment on her great use of dynamics first. "I really liked how expressive you were with your use of dynamics, Jennie. That is a huge improvement from our last lesson; good for you! Let's try this section again and this time, I want you to concentrate more on keeping the tempo steady. I'll clap the beat with you to get us started…" In this situation, the student will come away from the lesson knowing what her strengths and weaknesses are without feeling either falsely praised or criticized too harshly.

There are obvious extremes to avoid. By all means, do not tell a child that they are the worst trumpet player you have ever heard and why don't they give up, but don't tell them that those eighth notes they played completely wrong sound beautiful either. The keys here are honesty, constructive guidance, and balance. Then, when your students actually *do* advance musically and sound like a million bucks, you'll compliment them genuinely, and your words will be meaningful. Compliments are like that special restaurant: if you go there too often, it doesn't mean as much.

October 5

Today was a tough day. The vocal field trip to a local college choral festival that I have been planning is finally confirmed after much phone tag, changing times, and calling bus companies. Getting that organized has kept me busy during the little prep time that I have to begin with. But in a way, it's been fun to put together my first field trip.

The real thorn in my side today was, of course, the Jazz Band. I immediately felt guilty for being sick on our last rehearsal day because they were horrible. I don't want to be really strict or hard on them, as it is not my nature, and I refuse to play easy, baby music with them. We have a performance in three weeks and I'm starting to get very nervous about it. I'm not sure how to get through to them—I could do music checks with them like I'm doing with the Chorus, but I feel we need the rehearsal time as a group to gel together. After I went home today, I felt the worst I think I have in my entire life: bad day at school, still a little sick, allergies, whole body hurting, and sick of being worn out all the time. I need to know how to deal with all of this better.

October 6

I'm very happy that today is Friday—this has been a tough week for me. Talked with Dr. V. about my feelings dealing with my low energy and I'm really glad I did. She said that it was completely normal and that I was doing fine. It helped me a lot to hear that.

As the year moves ahead and you get more used to your schedule, both your body and mind will recover. To help things along, eat healthy, drink lots of water, and exercise. Even if you are drained to the limit, try to take a little walk to get some fresh air after a long day at school. You really will feel better.

> Late in the school day and after school were interesting. During last hour, I talked with a girl from Chorus who was curious about her grade. After we discussed that, she asked if she could stay down in the music area and not go back to study hall because apparently she is having some problems with certain boys harassing her. She said she told guidance and it is being dealt with, but I also told her if she needed anything else to let me know.
>
> Also had to talk with the Color Guard about the conflicts they have been having. The captains are not being good leaders and all the girls have their own ideas of how things should be done. During camp, they had a coach, but now they have to be more self-guided. I want them to keep things as student-led as possible, but I was glad that they came to me for help. We talked some issues through and I advised them on a few decisions that needed to be made, such as which uniform they would wear for the local college parade this weekend. Personally, I think the whole problem was just pettiness among the girls. They are all friends, but only two of them are captains, so sometimes that creates some animosity.

Weekend – College Homecoming Parade and
City Marching Competition

   Busy weekend with the Marching Band—
hate to admit it, but by the end of everything,
I was kinda sick of them! But they did a
great job. They looked sharp during the
parade: a little fatigued toward the end, so
their lines slipped a bit. But the crowd loved
them - they were dancing along to our music!
   The marching show competition was a
good experience too. We were missing a few
kids so there were holes in the drill, but the
performance was one of our better ones. It
was organizationally tough and nerve-wracking
because the Band had never done a competition
like this before, even though our entry was
in the non-competitive exhibition class.
After we performed, we watched the rest
of the bands perform their drills—wow!
Seeing all of the public school bands, with
their huge enrollments, expensive equipment
and multitude of instructors made me very
jealous, not to mention the attitudes and
dedication of the students—there were no
holes in any of their drills! I want to work
toward those goals with my own program,
but I know that it will take time.

October 9

   Actually, today was a pretty good Monday,
considering that I really didn't have much

free time over the weekend. Productive
Jazz rehearsal—sounds like people practiced,
plus we worked on a little easier music (not
baby music yet!) to help boost their confi-
dence. Also had a very helpful conversation
with a parent over the weekend about the
history of the Jazz Band, so that greatly
aided me in understanding their behavior.
   Called some parents today of kids who
aren't doing too well in certain classes—to
give them warnings before first quarter
grades are due in a few weeks. I was pretty
scared to do it—nervous to talk with parents
like this for the first time, but it went fine.
All the parents were receptive, and I was
careful to comment on positives that I am
seeing from their kids as well as the things
they need to work on. It made me feel good
to connect with those parents and get more
perspective on their kids.

History! Here I was banging my head against a
wall for nearly two months about the Jazz Band,
when all I needed was a brief history lesson. The
Jazz Band never used to be an official class; rather,
the students got together on their own over lunch
or after school and had a "jam session." Only within
the last few years had it become a class led by a teacher
to take for credit. Combined with the knowledge
that their last director was extremely lax concerning
discipline and an efficient rehearsal atmosphere, it
is no wonder that the jazz students were used to

being disorganized and talkative.

Being aware of the history of the music department can be extremely valuable, particularly in situations like this one. This history does not excuse the students' inappropriate behavior, but it does explain it. In turn, I was able to deal with the problem more effectively. Personally, I was also reassured that the situation was not a result of my teaching methods.

So, what did I do with this new knowledge? How did my approach to this group change? Not much. Consistency and time would heal this situation. I needed to show the students that I was in it for the long haul, to stress that the betterment of the ensemble outweighed their need to socialize at that exact moment. I wanted them to really experience learning about important jazz concepts, such as rhythms and articulations, and not merely treat class as a garage band get-together. I wanted to show them that I cared about helping them become a better jazz band. And it worked. Improvements were gradual, of course, and the students' attention spans slipped sometimes, but by the end of the school year we really grew as an ensemble: and as a team more disciplined and confident about the effective ways to reach our musical goals.

October 13

    Last couple days have been very busy, and not necessarily with current things, but

planning for things that are two or three
weeks away: set-up for choral concert, bus
for Jazz Band performance at a local convention, open house night at school, permission
slips for vocal field trip, etc. It feels like
these things keep me busier than actual
teaching—I need a secretary!

Sometimes it's hard to find the "special
moments" in the everyday routine. I guess I
just don't feel a heightened sense of purpose
in collecting permission slips. That's something the college professors don't tell you:
that not every moment of your day as an
educator will be wonderful and enlightening....

As far as tonight being the last home
football game and Marching Band performance, frankly I'm glad it's over. Anxious for
the focus to change to Concert Band. As fun
as Marching Band is, I'm a little sick of
yelling and being so "yay, rah rah, go team!"
all the time. Plus the kids got more irrespon-
sible as the season went on, which I can't
figure out. We kept improving in our drill
and performances, but at this last game,
about six or seven kids lost or forgot their
gloves—irritating. They want to be treated
like adults, but they act like 5-year olds
sometimes. How do you teach responsibility?

If you can answer that question, please let me in
on the secret!

October 16

This was really the first Monday of the school year that felt like a stereotypical "Monday" for me. I had to work hard to get myself psyched up for the day. Plus, I totally screwed up in Fundamentals. I had the right idea—we were doing some activities at the board and I started them out simply by having them draw treble clefs and basic musical notation. But then I jumped too far ahead into difficult major and minor keys instead of going through easier keys or the circle of fifths first. They got very confused and frustrated. But in a way I felt good about it because I know that this is something that none of them know, even with their varied musical abilities, so none of them should have an excuse to be bored...maybe. Also found some pages in one of my old theory books to copy and make a packet of information for them, so the lesson will be more concrete next time.

Keep in mind: as a first-year teacher fresh out of college, many things will seem easy for you that will dumbfound your students. For example, as a music major in college, you eat, sleep, and breathe major and minor scales. In the journal entry above, I needed to go a lot slower on this topic than I was prepared for. Don't lapse back into your college choral rehearsals or your university theory class. It is easy to do though, since it's the environment you were used for so long (some of us for longer than others...). Do not feel bad about having to remind yourself of what level your students are at. Keep them challenged, but not lost.

October 17

   PSAT test today, so for half the day, I was missing many of my kids from class. And I discovered the first school employee that I really didn't care for: a guidance counselor that talks to kids like they're idiots and asked me to give my musicians a study hall so the music wouldn't disturb the kids testing across the hall—grrr—what nerve! Anyway, had my rehearsals, though I probably wasn't very professional when I rehearsed some particularly loud sections of music over and over...or when I complained about the incident to some kids—have to keep that professional distance. One of the first Concert Band rehearsals since the switch from Marching Band and my two trombone players have already lost their music...again with the responsibility!

October 19

   Open house tonight and field trip tomorrow, so getting final details organized both musically and non-musically. Lots to think about. Chorus improving—piano player needs to practice lots more, but in general, the kids

are remembering more. Still amazing to me
the difference between them and Show
Choir—for the Show Choir, all their songs
for the musical revue are assigned and they
are rehearsing on their own in addition to
our class time together.

Good String Ensemble rehearsal—at the
beginning of the year, I would never hear a
peep of conversation from them, but now a
few gabbers are emerging. I guess it's sort
of good because they must feel comfortable,
but I don't want a lax atmosphere. Good
flute sectional, but the clarinets couldn't
count in theirs. Sometimes I get so frustrated
when I have to rehearse things over and
over, so I have to work on that. I know how
to go through the process with them and
when they actually get it, it's rewarding, so
I need to remember that.

The open house is an important tool for
the school to recruit eighth grade students
and their families to enroll in our high
school for next year. All the departments
put on displays, administration speaks, and
families tour around the building. As I spoke
with many middle school students and their
parents about the music department, the
evening flew by. I asked music students to
volunteer their time to come in and practice
in order to fill the rooms up with music.
Teachers and administration said that it was
a nice display, but I'm not sure how effective
it was for families to see only small groups
or individuals practicing.

In a private school, recruiting students is essential to our livelihood. Families need to be given solid reasons why they should pay five thousand dollars per year to send their child to our school. Students need to feel excited and challenged by all of the various opportunities the school will offer them. Moreover, the feelings that families and children receive about music, art, drama, or other elective subjects often determines their decision about which school to choose, because quality in these areas is vitally important to the entire school's educational atmosphere. It is also very meaningful to many young people socially and personally. I would guess that statements such as, "That school didn't have a choral music program," are usually more common reasons for a family not to attend a school than, "I didn't like that one math teacher we met."

It is for these reasons that I feel recruitment tools like school open houses are especially necessary for a developing music program, both in a private or public school setting. In a sense, you are a salesperson. You want to "sell" your department so students "buy" and come to build your program. It is a great opportunity to showcase your students' talents and the quality of your department to a receptive audience. What better way to explain to prospective students and parents what you do in your music department than to show them? After they have visited, count on prospective parents telling neighbors and other parents about the great (or mediocre) things happening in your music department. In this way, you reach people that were not even present at the event. Good old "word-of- mouth" works wonders...or could be devastating. Take your responsibilities concerning these public relations events very seriously, as your behavior, attitude, and personality directly affect the enrollment of your department. Surely you are not the only factor making or breaking the music program, but do not underestimate your powerful influence.

I have a ton of new and better ideas to incorporate into the open house next year. First of all, there will be a second music teacher, so that will help from the start. One teacher can be talking with parents, and the other can be working on my second idea, which is to have *entire* groups rehearsing, putting on a five-minute slice of what a typical music class is like. I can have a video showing tapes of concerts. I can have a flyer printed with pertinent information about the music department for students and parents to take home for a reference. This is merely the beginning of ideas for this type of situation. Try to think of some more of your own!

October 20

Choir field trip day! An hour long bus ride to an area college for a choir festival—singing and getting critiqued by a college professor, tour of campus, lunch, etc. Kids behaved and

> sang very well—I thought that it would be a
> lot more stressful than it was, but they were
> all on task, on time, and where they were
> supposed to be. Everyone was accounted for
> the several times I took attendance, they
> had good attitudes, behaved on the buses,
> etc. It helped to have the three parent
> chaperones along for extra sets of eyes and
> ears, as it would've been pretty overwhelm-
> ing to look after 80 kids all by myself. The
> clinic itself was a good experience, too. The
> professor gave a lot of helpful ideas to all
> the ensembles about diction, breath support,
> and phrasing. It was time-consuming to col-
> lect permission slips, money, and in general
> to organize the trip, but it was worth it.
> And the day went so fast...

Your field trip can also go this smoothly if you remember some simple guidelines. First and foremost, like I've mentioned before, be organized. Have an accurate list of students and check it often. Know the itinerary for the day and share it with your students and chaperones so they also understand what to expect. When you are planning this itinerary, make sure that there is very little "down time." Your field trip should be full of constant activity. Obviously, kids need time to visit the restroom, but having too much free time will increase their potential for getting into trouble.

My next advice depends on the age and maturity

level of the group; however, almost any child should be able to handle this concept to some degree. Stress to your students the importance of *being responsible for their own behavior.* A field trip, whether it is completely for fun or going to a clinic like my choirs did in the above example, is a privilege. As I revealed in my journal entries, it is also a lot of work for you as the teacher. If your students choose to break the trust you have placed in them and behave irresponsibly, make sure they know the consequences of their actions.

October 23

Very busy Monday—preparing to be gone on Thursday and Friday to the annual Music Convention in Madison, but we have two performances on Sunday—Jazz Band at a local convention and the fall choral concert. I'm nervous about only seeing some of the groups once this week, then having that performance. Organizing substitute lesson plans, typing concert programs, etc.

I'm worried about the Chorus. As a whole, they're okay, but their accompanist is not. He only has one of their three songs even close to being ready to play at the performance! I finally gave copies of the music to an upperclassmen pianist and said if I can't count on this student to get the job done, he might have to fill in. Like I need this stress in addition to everything else that's

---

going on right now. Since it's close to the end of the first quarter, lots of kids are worried about their grades. I have to start thinking about completing all the grades on the computer program; hopefully there won't be any weird malfunctions. I'm not even 100% sure how to run the program...another one of those things that no one fills you in on....

Band was a challenge again today. Some of the students just will not be quiet. We waste so much time in rehearsal. I try to be as organized and down-to-business as possible, and still things are not getting better. Also today was the first day that a band student really smarted off to me. I purposely tried not to react too harshly and handled it calmly, to prove that wasn't the way to get my attention. Later in rehearsal, I asked him a question about the music we were working on to try and show that I was "moving on," so I hope that helped.

On a different topic, my uncle passed away a few days ago. I told the office about it and it was announced and prayed for during the morning prayer. I had lots of kids come up to me today and say that they were sorry, which was really touching.

October 24 – My Birthday!

Interesting to have my "golden birthday" be my first birthday in a career. Mostly, the day was very sweet. The Concert Choir sang "Happy Birthday" to me and I received cards and a monster-sized chocolate kiss in my mailbox in the office.

The end of the day was more stressful than I would've liked to deal with on my birthday, though. The copy machine was down, so I couldn't copy the program for the choir concert. Mom and Dad traveled from out of town and showed up at school, so that was cool, but I also felt really bad and stressed because I had so much to do that I couldn't stop and talk with them until after I met them later for dinner. Still getting ready to go to the convention on Thursday—there was a snag with the payment and registration, so had to straighten that out, plus finalize sub plans, etc. The stuff that seems very extracurricular to actual classroom teaching is very difficult to find the time to deal with sometimes.

The music convention that I attended at the end of October was a marvelous experience for me and would be for any first-year teacher. I attended the convention as a college student, but to be there as a professional was so much more meaningful and enlightening. It was very interesting to listen to speakers, go to presentations, and see exhibits after actually being in the field of education.

There are many reasons to attend educational conventions, not the least of which being the free merchandise you receive from vendors and the free samples of food from all the fundraising companies!

These exhibits are fun, plus give some great ideas for materials, products, and music to use in your program. I saw many friends, past teachers, and colleagues during the convention. It was insightful to talk with them about our common experiences and created for me a sense of camaraderie with my fellow music directors from around the state. With speakers making brilliant presentations on many different topics concerning the music education world and musical performances on all grade levels, it is easy to become inspired with new ideas. Teachers often take these new thoughts back to their classroom and try to incorporate them into their everyday instructional techniques. Don't think that conventions "brainwash" educators and take away all of their personal ideas; they make good teachers better teachers.

For me, the biggest thing that the convention did was give me back my spark. Through the five years or more of college, student teaching, and interviewing, young people are filled with that zest to teach and "make a difference." After two months on the front lines of education, much of that may be buried under paperwork, behavior, and everyday life. These are normal feelings, but don't let them keep you down. Attending a convention may not be a cure-all, but it does offer all of the above possibilities. Plus it gives teachers a break from the routine, something often underestimated. Everyone in every profession needs that sometimes in order to recharge and regain focus.

October 29 – Sunday – Jazz Performance
and Choir Concert

I can't believe how fast today went! And
how smoothly! The Jazz performance at the
local church and family convention was a lot
of fun. As we were background music in the
restaurant area, it was not too stressful.
We played well, set up efficiently, and pleased
the crowd. It was also great to talk to the
Jazz kids during the bus ride to the performance. I wish that I had more time during
the normal school day to just simply talk
with students.

After that, I rushed over to the college
where the fall choral concert was going to
be. I was very nervous, since this was my
first formal concert performance. I was
not only nervous about the quality of the
performance, but also the organizational
aspects that a concert presents, like moving
the groups on and off stage, etc. Since I
was never in this college concert hall that
we use for school performances, the set-up
and logistics of it kept me on edge....

Most kids arrived when they were supposed
to: an hour before the performance. We warmed
up and walked through the order of the concert. They were cooperative, but a little too
chatty. Parents and friends started filing in
and before I knew it, it was show time.
Everything I worried about, especially the
flow of the concert, turned out great. Even

the students who read the announcements
introducing the pieces did well. I enjoyed
lots of compliments and the knowledge that
my first formal concert was now under my belt.

If you are a teacher who puts on performances at a facility outside of your school, which is probably almost all of us at some time or another, this reflection is for you. There are many stresses involved in making a successful concert in your own facility, not to mention somewhere else. I have a few friendly tips to make your remote performance a success. First of all, communicate regularly with the correct people. At the college where we hold our concerts, there is a lovely lady who bears the title of "Facilities Coordinator." I speak with her whenever I need to reserve the auditorium, and she sends me a contract, which holds and confirms our concert dates. Later, about two weeks before the actual performance date, I call her again to give her the set-up of how many chairs, stands, risers, or percussion equipment we need for the concert. The work order is written down and the stage is set up for us when we arrive. Most off-campus performance events or facilities will have some sort of organizational system like this, and usually it works well. I would still suggest arriving early to make sure everything is in order. Lastly, impress upon your students the importance of treating the facility with respect.

October 30

  Felt pretty good going back to school today after the Music Convention and great performances. I brought in a pumpkin to decorate my office, so that put a smile on my face as well.

  Had a conversation with the Chorus, with my hope being that it would be a friendly discussion about positives and negatives from yesterday's performance. But that was not how it happened. Several students were very outspoken in their complaints about the music we sang; they didn't like it. Most kids were fine; they either had positive things to say, constructive criticism, or they defended the music. It was interesting to me how most of the complaints came from people who usually don't sing or pay attention anyway. Maybe they don't realize that I might be more willing to bargain with them if they took the class seriously. They want to sing pop songs all the time, which I don't think is best for their total learning experience. They say they want choices about which pieces we sing, but why should I give them choices when they don't work with me in the first place? Would that reinforce their inappropriate behavior? I wonder what I should do? Should I go with their wishes, or is that bribing them to pay attention? Why should I give them harder music and let them snap or move to the beat if they can't sing their regular parts? I think that the conversation

was good to have, but the attacking tone of
voice from some of them was hard for me to
take... and I let them know that wasn't the
best way to communicate effectively. I did
take some of their advice and ordered "You're
a Mean One, Mr. Grinch" for the Christmas
Concert; hopefully, they see that as a fun song.
    Band had a good rehearsal today on
"Kilimanjaro: An African Portrait," and low
brass and percussion had productive sectionals. I felt confident for the first time
that we will be able to play that piece at our
fall concert in a few weeks. Grades on my
computer are messed up and no one has really
been that helpful in telling me what I have
to do to fix them, so that's been stressful.

Time for a sneaky teacher trick. I think it's
important to give musical ensembles some choices
in the music they perform. As I mentioned in the
beginning of the year, I did it with the more advanced
choir. I knew that they could handle it. I think if I
would let the Chorus do that, we would only sing
arrangements by The Backstreet Boys or Madonna.
If you feel you want to give them choices, but still
want to perform certain pieces, do what I learned to
do later in the school year: mix in simply horrible
pieces of music with the ones that you want the
group to work on. Have a sight-reading day and dig
out some of the worst music your music library has
to offer. *You* know that you have no intention of

working on that horrendous piece, but *they* don't! They will most certainly end up voting for the music that you would've picked out anyway, plus they will feel good about it! Shush, don't tell them I told you….

October 31 – Halloween

Fun day—kids and faculty dressed up, gave out candy, etc. Other than that, it was a spooky, horrible day for getting grades in. They were due yesterday, but I told the main office that I would get them in today and they still called my office all day to bother me. I had to wait for the Fundamentals oral presentations and that class is toward the end of the day, plus I still had to enter concert grades from the past weekend performances. Anyway, then my computer went nuts. First, I never knew that I had to do grades on the A drive instead of the C drive, and they couldn't be transferred from one to the other. I just about cried; I had to start all over. Then, the disk didn't work. The computer lady came down to my office and ended up having to replace the entire disk drive. Yuck! Stressful, but I finally got them done after working like crazy between classes and for a long time after school. It was extremely difficult to focus on teaching my classes when I had this grading problem on my mind all day—very distracting.

So, by the end of October, a quarter of the school year is behind you. By now, it may seem like you've done everything at least once: grades, concerts, phone calls home to parents, field trips, conventions, ordering music, meetings with the principal, and a sick day to top it all off. It feels good to have all of those experiences "figured out." Maybe you think that since you've made it this far, the rest of the school year will be a breeze. What else could possibly come along to throw your world for a loop? I'm so glad you asked....

November

I didn't realize just how crazy a music director's life could get until I experienced November. You may be thinking, what the heck happens in November to make life so stressful? Plenty. Not only are you working with the students on fall music and activities, but you are also starting to make the shift to Christmas and holiday programs. You begin to realize how little time you have to accomplish a whole lot of events, from concerts to parent/teacher conferences. In fact, this month, I dealt with some of toughest things of the entire school year. But I had some great moments performing and teaching, too. I felt like I really grew a lot as an educator and a human being in November.

November 2

Crappy Jazz rehearsal today. I just don't know how else to explain the concepts of this one piece we've been working on. We never end the chart together, so I slowed the tempo down, sang parts to them and separated the different sections and nothing has helped much. What we really need is for them to go home and practice the things we work on so they don't forget them by next rehearsal again. Even though we have been slowly getting better and more organized, today they were extremely chatty. For the first time, I yelled (more like screamed like a crazed lunatic) at them to shut up to start rehearsal. I know it was surprising for them because I never do that. In fact, I surprised myself! I hate yelling, but I think they just needed that today.

Started some Christmas music with the Concert Choir. That was fun and went well. I also started programs on the computer for the fall instrumental concert.

November 3

Good Chorus rehearsal today—still more talking than I would like, but they all really seemed to be into the music. The "Grinch" song was a hit, plus I did some different warm-ups with them. Sometimes it's easy to forget that the students need variety to keep things fresh.

Ran through the whole program with the String Ensemble for their performance at the fall concert. Got good feedback from them about how they played and how it felt to run everything through without stopping, so that was neat. Great Concert Band rehearsal—felt like I really did a great job teaching and conducting today. Show Choir is also moving right along. They are learning their pieces for the musical revue quickly and beginning to add dance moves and choreography.

On this particular day, I think that one of the reasons Concert Band went so well was my use of *analogies*. I realized quickly that analogies were something that kids respond to very well and I encourage their use whenever possible. However, like anything, if you overuse them, they are not as effective; that's why you have to think of many different ones!

The two analogies I used that day in rehearsal seemed to "strike the right chord" with the kids and they really understood what I was trying to get at. The first one I used was when the students really didn't sound like they were "into" the music. The sounds they were making sounded tired and lethargic. I stopped them and asked, "What day is it today?" After a few goofy looks, they all said that it was Friday. I replied, "Well, you guys are playing like it's a Monday! Your collective sound is very tired and bummed out. I want you to play like it's a Friday and you're excited about the weekend! Smiles! Lots of happiness, sleeping in, going out—let's hear that! Okay, here we go…" When they started playing again, their sound was much more upbeat, energetic, and focused, which was exactly what I wanted.

While the first analogy I used was more mental, the second one was physical. The band was having a very difficult time doing a crescendo exactly the way I wanted. To be more specific, they were getting loud too quickly instead of gradually growing into the larger volume. So, I had them stand up…two different ways. First, I asked them to stand up very quickly (being careful not to drop instruments or send music stands flying, of course). The second time, I asked them to stand up as slowly as they could, feeling the constant motion, the tension in their muscles, the growth to their full height. I explained to them that we were doing the crescendo similar to how we stood up the first way—getting to our full volume too soon. I wanted us to do the crescendo the second way, focusing fully on the growth and expansion of the sound, just like they did physically with their bodies. We tried it…and it worked beautifully! I received the best crescendo of the entire year! Making those special parallels and connections to get your point across is often the difference between your students merely playing the music and having them feel and understand it.

November 6

Very frustrating beginning of the day— the Chamber Ensemble had a bad rehearsal. My most talented student was gone and the rest couldn't keep time on this march arrange- ment we are working on for the fall concert. I guess what people say about marches is true sometimes: they are easy to play, but difficult to play well. I got crabby with the kids. It was probably not the best answer, but I needed to let them know that I was disappointed. Worked on rhythms with new

pieces in Concert Choir. I am trying to get
them to read the music and really figure out
the notes, rhythms, etc. instead of just echoing
what I sing or play. I asked for volunteers
to try the difficult rhythms and no one said
a word.

Hear ye, hear ye. Apparently, sometimes the quickest way to quiet down a high school classroom is to question the class and ask for a response. If you want to hear a pin drop, ask for volunteers!

Better Jazz Ensemble rehearsal today.
The rhythm section was more "with it" and
our pieces were coming together well. Also
good Fundamentals class—reviewed theory
concepts we started before quarter presentations. I still have one student who needs
to do his presentation (note how long it has
been since the end of the first quarter) and
he was magically not here again today.
Irritating. I am trying, with everything else,
to teach kids responsibility, punctuality,
getting things done, etc. So when they don't
understand that, it bothers me. I am trying
to help them out now, and for their future
in the real world, and it's like they don't
want my help.

November 7

Getting ready for fall instrumental concert in five days. I'm working on finishing the program and announcements for students to read. This week, we've been having bigger sectionals instead of rehearsing with only the flutes or trumpets at one time. Today, I combined the flutes and clarinets together, as well as the saxes and trumpets. Seemed to be productive, going to do another one next A Day. I'm glad that most of them have been flexible and cooperative in attending these sectionals, as they are out of the ordinary and some of them have to be excused from their study hall or eat lunch at a different time.

Something that has been bothering me: I wish that I wouldn't have to do so many announcements at the beginning of class, Band especially, and "waste" our valuable rehearsal time. But how else can I get them the info they need?

Separated into sectionals all hour for the String Ensemble— trying to especially help the second violins get their parts down better. I think that it was helpful; I guess we'll see in our final rehearsal before the concert.

It was at this point in the year that some things about my teaching began to bother me. Not necessarily concerns about efficiency, like the "announcements before class" dilemma, but things that I knew were becoming bad habits. I think that I didn't notice them before because I was just too wrapped up in dealing with being a new teacher. I'm embarrassed to admit that it took me this long to step outside of myself and really be aware of two of my big weaknesses, but better late than never. In fact, I still battle them, as do many music teachers, young and old.

The first annoyance was keeping my eyes buried in the score while I was conducting. I was comfortable with the conducting gestures of my hands, arms, and body language in general, but I was not looking up at the kids in the ensembles nearly enough. I'm sure that you were told in your conducting classes in college how important eye contact is with a musical ensemble. But perhaps you weren't told just how difficult it is. You may not realize it, but by making eye contact with a group of fifteen, fifty, or two hundred people, you make yourself vulnerable. For those of us who are closer to shy on the continuum from shy to outgoing, that can be a nightmare. A new piece, a new teaching position with a new group of musicians, or even just a bad day can cause a loss of self-assurance and poor eye contact, even for directors who are more outgoing or confident.

The reasons why eye contact as a musical director is important are numerous; however, you only need to know one. Any lack of confidence on your part will result in substandard performances from your ensembles. Students need to have the guarantee that they can look up to the podium for direction and assurance. If they don't have that, they falter.

My second habit is that I say the word "guys" *a lot*. "Guys, let's get started," and, "Guys, that was really good!" are just a few examples. I think that many teachers have a word or phrase that sneaks into their vocabulary more than they would like. What makes mine even more embarrassing for me is that my friends and I made fun of a teacher at the high school I attended who said "guys" all the time. I guess the fates are getting even with me!

You may not think that a habit like this is very harmful and to some extent, you are right. Although it is common, this is definitely not one of big serious offenses of the education profession. In fact, if this is one of your only problems, especially as a first-year teacher, you are probably doing very well. But what this habit does is threaten your credibility and affect how seriously your students take you, which is indeed a big consideration.

The good news is there are simple solutions to these shortcomings in your teaching. The first step is to merely recognize the problem; once you are aware of it, you can do something about it. Keep a journal—really try to be honest with yourself about how good or bad your (fill-in-the-blank-habit) was that day and vow to improve it the next day. Maybe you can even improve it as you are teaching. I've become so aware of my eye contact and conducting habits that now I automatically know when I have not been looking at the students enough, so I correct it right at that moment. Ask a colleague or your principal to observe you, watching for certain quirks. One of the rehearsals my principal observed, she tallied up my "guys" count…thirteen. Ouch. That score-keeping sticks in my mind when I am addressing groups and helps me remove it from my vocabulary. Visit with a college professor or a veteran music director in the area and ask for their input and advice. Set up a video camera in the back of the room, focused on you instead of the students to record your progress. We ask our students to keep striving for improvements; we should demand the same from ourselves as their instructors.

November 9

All of the last rehearsals before this Sunday's instrumental concert were fine; it's Thursday though, and we have tomorrow off. Next year, I will have to schedule concerts more effectively because I don't like that we have Friday off before a concert. Allows for too many brain lapses. I have been busy with other things too: sent out letters to all parents letting them know about the new Band Parent Committee that several other parents want to start, ordered some music for solo and ensemble festival, and obviously have been thinking ahead to Christmas concert music and rehearsals.

November 12 - Fall Instrumental Concert

   Right before I stepped onto stage to begin the concert, I was so nervous I was shaking! I closed my eyes, took a few deep breaths and went over the music, as well as the previous two hours in my head. I was glad that I got to the auditorium early because the percussion equipment was not set up for us like it should have been. So I had to call the college campus security to have them come over and open the stage storage room, then I set up all the instruments myself. But I got it all done and also put the programs and donation box out by the entrance. Then I tried to center myself after a stressful beginning to the day.
   The students arrived relatively on time, but I still didn't feel focused. I wish that I would've done even more tuning and warm-ups with them than I did. I was worried about the time and organization of the concert. The musicians were sitting in their spots quietly and listening attentively...and I was such a wreck that I didn't have much to say to them! Darn! I wish I would've been more inspiring and encouraging also.
   It was show time. It was time to put all of the worries of the last hour or so behind me and do the best job I could. After a quiet calming smile to myself and a deep breath, I walked confidently out onto stage and took my place at the podium. I presented the group a public smile as a student recited

the introduction. I gave the first downbeat, and from there, the concert soared. There were some minor mistakes, as there almost always are, but everyone was great and the program flowed along smoothly. There were great dynamics and emotional involvement from the ensembles. I felt that my conducting could've been better, but for my first instrumental concert, I was happy. After every piece, there was always lots of applause. My parents were able to be there; my dad brought flowers to me up on stage at the end! Several students' parents shared some very complimentary comments afterwards, which made me feel like a million bucks! I wish that I had more time to relax and enjoy this success, but I feel like I have to be working right away tomorrow on other things.

November 13

I tried to enjoy today and take a deep breath after yesterday's success, but still have to keep moving forward. The big job now is getting the instrumental groups focused on Christmas music and started on it right away with that concert being December 10th.

As you may remember, when I first took my new job, there were no concerts scheduled on the school calendar. It was difficult to reserve the nearby college auditorium for *any* dates, much less ones that were convenient or left ample time in which to prepare concerts. Take the scheduling of your concert dates very seriously, especially your first year of teaching. Make sure you give yourself and your ensembles plenty of time to rehearse effectively for performances. In my situation, I didn't have that luxury, but I knew what I could do to make the situation better in the future. For the following year, I scheduled our concerts in April, a full three months before I was even hired my first year! I purposely did things like carefully checking the school calendar and leaving more time in between the fall and Christmas concerts. Hopefully, it will work better; I made every effort to try. Your concerts are one of the most visual and public things you will do as a music teacher. Help them to work for you as a fun showcasing of your students' talent, not against you as a stressor or something to dread.

> Negative attitudes really affected me today; I thought that the kids would be happy after their concert. When I handed out Christmas music to the Jazz Band, one of my saxophones made a comment about a particular piece: "If we couldn't play this

last year, why could we this year?" (I felt like saying, "Maybe because you're all a year older, hopefully better musicians, and because I say we can?) I really had to hold my tongue. That comment shot me down because if they have that attitude, it will be very hard to succeed. I'm not going to let them think that—I'm gonna try to let that comment challenge me to teach the piece to the absolute best of my ability.

November 14

I felt overwhelmed today with everything that is coming up: pep rally, parent/teacher conferences, Strings field trip to play at a benefit luncheon, student assistance day, the city Christmas parade, the Show Choir musical revue, and the Christmas concert are all less than a month away. Band watched the video of the fall concert. I gave them an evaluation sheet to fill out to get their thoughts and comments. The kids listened pretty well and wrote some really insightful things. After I've read all of them, I will give them back so they can keep the sheets in their folders like a journal. I think it will help them monitor their progress and it gives them some ownership and responsibility. Almost all of the kids said that they have to practice more, so I hope that hits home and they actually do what they know they need to do.

November 15

   Wednesday and last "real" class day of
the week with conferences and string outing
tomorrow and student assistance day on
Friday. Getting started with Chamber Ensemble
and Jazz Band on Christmas music—I can't
believe how fast it will come and how few
rehearsals we have until then. These two
groups also watched and critiqued the fall
concert tape. Jazz did a whole lot worse
than I thought—at least that's how it sounded
on the tape...and I guess they don't lie. They
were out of tune, blasty, and not tight together
at all with rhythms, missed notes, etc. They
heard it and they weren't pleased either, so
maybe that will motivate them to do better.

Truth hurts. But it did them good in the long run.

November 16

   The kids had the day off from school
because of parent/teacher conferences taking
up the entire day. I thought that the String
Ensemble might resent giving half of their
day off to play background music at a benefit
luncheon, but they loved it! It was actually
something that I received a phone call about
a few months ago and looked forward to ever
since. Besides, getting out of a few hours of

conferences didn't sound bad, either.

It was a great performance for us and also a wonderful experience overall. We played in the lobby of a beautiful reception center where people drank wine, strolled along, and listened to us play. With an expected turnout of around six hundred people, the exposure for the group and the feeling of playing in front of that many people was incredible! Before everyone arrived, when the kids heard that number, eyes widened and nervous comments flew. But as they played, I watched them with my conductor's gaze and knew they were enjoying themselves.

A great experience. But perhaps even more important for the string ensemble was the pizza lunch they had after we were done performing. Maybe not as important from a music perspective, but from a human one. It was the first social thing, outside of school, that the group did together and I know that it was fun and bonding for them. As the school year progressed, I saw new friendships forming, comfort levels rising, and the common link of a musical adventure that made them a closer group. There are certainly other ways for students to bond together: camp for the marching band, or a field trip for the choirs. But I do recommend taking your students out for a public performance and some social time if your school and schedule allows. It is a very different musical atmosphere than playing at a school-sponsored event, and the kids get to see each other in a new environment, both of which are valuable experiences for young people as musicians and as people. Plus, getting your musical groups to play at an event like this gets your school's name and the good things you are doing out into the community.

When I returned to school after the string performance, I manned my table in the cafeteria for parent/teacher conferences. As you would expect, I felt very nervous and uneasy about this new situation. I had illusions of parents screaming at me, demanding that their child's grade be changed, ranting about the music I chose for the last concert, or insisting that I was a poor instructor. These nightmare-like scenarios played through my head like a skipping record, and I had no defense against their accusations. I envisioned myself crying like a child or facing off in a yelling match. Just as I became sure that I was doomed, my first parent walked over to my table.

For the most part, my lunatic predictions were completely wrong. Most of my talks with parents were very pleasant and positive. Many parents reported their happiness with the music program, which made me feel much more at ease with conferences and just plain happy about my hard work. However, there were a few meetings that were less than cheery.

I had a mother tell me that band should be an "easy A" for her son and if I was going to continue to give him B's, that she would have him drop the class and take a study hall instead. I personally was ruining her freshman son's chances of getting into Harvard, didn't I know? I had another parent insist that I should be calling him at home or work to tell him what his child's assignments were. I had yet another mother ask me, with daggers in her voice, "What can we do about my son's grade?"

Let me give you some defenses against comments like these. Some of these remarks I came up with, by some miracle, during my first year of teaching. Others I have learned over time. First of all, I don't believe that band or any other performing music class should be an "easy A." What a degrading way to think about such a beautiful thing as music. We like to believe that music is fun, and of course most students are in the group because they want to be, but that should not justify everyone getting A's on their report card. A performing music class requires hard work, dedication, listening skills, teamwork, knowing one's music and performing it to the best of one's ability, etc. And that's the short list. Parents often do not realize that if you would simply "give" everyone A's, even if students do not deserve them, the standards of the group would plunge dramatically. (Then these same parents would yell at you again, demanding to know why the band, orchestra, or choir stinks so badly!)

Standards and requirements in a performing musical ensemble, such as quality participation and musical cognition, are just as tough to meet, if not more so, than meeting criteria for an A in any other class. Music classes are often seen as "extra-curricular," even though they meet during the school day. Because music often involves activities such as concerts outside of the regular school schedule, it is sometimes viewed as fun and games; therefore not as structured or important as other classes. This is a misconception we must all fight to correct. Music is an *academic* area, where students are learning valuable skills, just like the "core" classes of any school. If a student does not get an A in history, I don't believe that very often a parent would go up to the history teacher and say, "History should be an easy A for my child, you must be doing something wrong."

When a student receives a less than desirable grade in history, math, science, or other required classes, those teachers are ready to explain to parents what the child can do to improve their grade *with concrete examples.* Advice such as "know your vocabulary more thoroughly," "keep a more organized lab notebook," or, "turn in your essays on time" can be heard often. As teachers of a performance-based class, our advice may be more abstract, but it is still vitally important to a child's growth and development... and of course, their grade. "Mrs. G., I know that Stephen's grade was not what you were expecting, but let me tell you how he *earned* this grade." (Grades are not *given,* they are *earned*). You are now free to elaborate about whatever Stephen's problems may be. Whether he doesn't know his music, doesn't pay attention in class, or doesn't take care of equipment, do not be shy in pointing out your observations. I suggest having everything very documented, such as marks in a grade book for missed lessons or talking during rehearsal. Yes, the paperwork and memory logistics of this are often difficult. No, I don't expect you to stop rehearsal so you can put a check by Stephen's name. However, think about a parent asking you, "Well, fine then, just how often does he talk during class?" and you not having a concrete answer. You must be able to justify all the grades you give, not just for the sake of parents or principals, but for your own integrity.

So, some tips thus far for surviving parent/teacher conferences are to keep accurate records of your students' grades and participation, stress that grades are earned, not given, and give parents concrete examples of how their student can improve. Another thing I would like to add here is to plan at least one positive comment for every student. Parents love to hear great things about their kids, so even if it is something as simple as "Matt has perfect attendance in my class" (he may not actually do anything while he's there, but you can get to that), it will get parents thinking more positively. As far as the parents who want you to call them every day with an update on everything going on in class, I think that's bogus. I am speaking from a high school perspective here; high school students should be mature enough to keep track of their own assignments without their teachers having to call Mommy and Daddy. If they cannot, perhaps they haven't been given the practice of being responsible where they should've been in the first place—home. And the mother who wanted to know what *we* could do about her son's grade…you guessed it—nothing. The question is, what can *he* do about his grade. Stressing responsibility as one of your criteria for success will help cultivate more accountable students. This not only helps them succeed in your class, but in other classes in school and ultimately through their entire life. They'll thank you later.

November 17 - Student Assistance Day

Student Assistance Day, cleverly scheduled the day after conferences, is really a day for students who are struggling in certain classes. If requested by the teacher, they come in to receive more individual attention, do make up work or a test, or other things deemed necessary. I think that I broke the mold a little bit when I required everyone in the Concert Band, Jazz Band, String Ensemble and Show Choir to come in for extra rehearsals. With so many things coming up, it seemed like a great way to get another rehearsal under our belts. It was a very busy and involved day, almost instantly moving from an hour with one group to an hour with the next. S.A. day generally only lasts until noon, and by then, I felt like I put an entire day in! But it went smoothly and was indeed very beneficial.

November 19 – Sunday –
City Christmas Parade

The first part of this late afternoon was like something directly out of "A Charlie Brown Christmas," with me playing the part of the disaster-prone Charlie Brown. I ordered a bus several weeks ago to pick the Marching Band up from school, drive us to the beginning of the parade route, and pick us up at the end. After waiting about 20 minutes past the designated arrival time, it was becoming painfully clear that the bus was not going to show, even with the several frantic phone calls I made to the clueless bus company secretary. Luckily, enough parents and kids with cars were able to shuttle everyone and their instruments to our meeting spot for the parade and take care of every-one afterwards. That was very nerve-wracking, but the parade itself was great. Marching at the band's side was a very different experience than watching them from the sidelines at our half-time shows: as I followed in step, I felt more involved. I felt honored to march alongside the band—they made me very proud. All of the rehearsals we spent marching

down the neighborhood streets surrounding
the school, lately freezing our tails off,
were proving worthwhile. It was cold and
snowy tonight, but crowd response was good
and marching through the decorated down-
town was beautiful.

"All I Ever Needed To Know About Bus Companies
I Learned on a Snowy Night." After this "freak acci-
dent" (at least that was what the bus company called
it), I learned to always call a few days before the
event to double check on the reservation, even if
they sent me a confirmation. That was what happened in this situation; they sent me a confirmation
letter, but the booking apparently was not written
down on their "main assignment board." Needless
to say, I will be taking my bussing business elsewhere.

November 20

Only have school on Monday and Tuesday
this week because of Thanksgiving, so want
to make everything as productive as possible. Chorus, Band, and String rehearsals all
fine—tried to at least touch on all of the
pieces. I stressed personal practice over
the break. After school and evening were
busy—supervised some of the Show Choir
rehearsal and in and out of Band parent

meeting talking about fund-raising for new uniforms. This Show Choir revue is just plain stressful. The kids are doing well, but I don't feel qualified enough to make them much better. I don't know enough about this theatre stuff. They have been doing a lot of choreography and rehearsing themselves while still under my supervision, which I think is great for their leadership skills, yet I don't feel like I have the control I should. I'm getting a weird vibe like they aren't happy with me, but I'm trying my best. Doing this project is not in my contract, so in a way I am doing this out of the goodness of my heart. I am giving up the little free time that I have to begin with—plus trying to not let it consume me or cause me to neglect my many other obligations.

November 21

Last day before Thanksgiving break and my trip to Atlanta with my beau to visit his family. The kids are pretty goofy. Don't ask me why the school decided to schedule a group picture day today, but the Marching Band had to get into full uniform for their yearbook picture. The kids knew about it in advance, but still were forgetting parts of their uniform, which I found ridiculous—how can they expect the rest of the school to take them seriously or to command respect if they act like that? I really let them have it—right in front of the photographers. Hopefully when and if we get those new uniforms next year they will treat them with more dignity.

I also spoke pretty sternly with the Concert Choir and the Jazz Band—they were so unfocused during rehearsal. Since this was such a short week and an important rehearsal before break, I felt their attention was even more crucial. In fact, I told the Jazz Band that anyone who wasn't serious about getting better and making good music could leave. Quality doesn't happen with lots of talking and screwing around. I was happy with my theory class—they finally understand major and minor key signatures. It was a cool feeling when they could answer tough questions aloud in class.

I don't know if my expectations for this class day before break were too high or not. What I do know is that it was not a very successful day. I was frustrated, the kids weren't centered and we were all antsy to get the heck out of school for a five-day break. I wanted the day to be productive, not to send many students and myself away on Thanksgiving vacation with negative feelings about our musical progress. I'm not sure what the "correct" answer is to avoid this situation. Maybe the rehearsal right before a few days off would be a good opportunity for a sectional rehearsal, to double-check rhythms, pitches and the like on a small group level, so that incorrect habits are not reinforced over a long weekend. Perhaps a full rehearsal is a good option, stressing segments of pieces that the ensemble already knows fairly well with the goal being to strengthen musicality. Maybe this is a video day, an opportunity for students to watch one of their previous performances, write a critique, and discuss goals for the rest of the school year. You should not have to lower your expectations, but I've found that the class day right before a vacation is not the most advantageous time to really push your students, as much as you may want to. Whatever your situation, I would advise trying many different things to discover what your particular group of students responds to most effectively.

The Monday after Thanksgiving break was one of the worst days of my first year of teaching. Not for petty reasons, like not being able to sleep in anymore or feeling fat from eating too much turkey, but because of an issue that temporarily broke my heart and spirit....

November 27

I have never felt so horrible about any aspect of teaching as I did today. There were Show Choir rehearsals over break which were supervised by another faculty member. I hoped that they would go smoothly, but I never imagined that I would encounter what I did. I came back from break Monday

---

morning to discover a venomous message on my school voice mail from a parent, blaming me for outrageous things. Apparently, some of the students were making fun of her daughter, which of course is bad enough in itself. But by having this faculty member supervise the rehearsals, whom I guess "hates" this woman's daughter and "allowed" the ridiculing to occur, made it look like I was out to get her daughter, too. She accused me of wanting to hurt her daughter on purpose. She charged me with not caring. She threatened my credibility as a teacher. Her accusations cut to the bone.

Luckily, I had a prep period and there were no students around, although I don't know if I could've done anything different, no matter what the circumstances. I started to sob. I didn't know what to do. As much as I could, I collected myself and called the office, asking if the principal, Dr. V., could come down to see me. I'm sure the secretary knew something was wrong, because my principal was down in my office in a flash. She sat by me, listened to the message and helped me through it. She said I didn't have to go through it alone. She listened to my feelings and frustrations and let me cry. It helped, but I still feel horrible. Maybe I should just "blow it off" and not take it so personally, but how can I? It was a real struggle to get through the day and stay focused.

An important lesson to learn: if a parent has given another teacher problems, they will probably find something to harass you about also, no matter how wonderful you try to be. I had been warned about this mother by other teachers—that she loved to stir up trouble and make false accusations. I thought, I'm going to be different. And for a while, I lived in that fantasy. This family began the year sweet and helpful, volunteering to help me with anything. Then they turned on me by questioning my integrity and accusing me of things I would never dream of. That was probably what made it hurt the most; the fact that they had been so great before. But I guess I should have expected it. They treated the last music director horribly. Plus, other content area teachers started telling me about the problems *they* had with these people. Hardly a trustworthy track record.

Maybe you've guessed already, but this situation can be boiled down to one word: *control*. People act the way they do for any number of reasons, but in my experience with obnoxious parents, most often the reason they get bent out of shape has to do with what level of control they have… or most likely don't have. I don't mean to sound insensitive to their daughter's problem with some of her classmates, but I think there is much more to the issue. This is only a theory I have, but the more I thought about it, the more it made sense to me. Like I stated, these parents helped me a great deal at the beginning of the school year. As I became more comfortable in my teaching role, I "needed" them less and less. As the school year progressed, I met more parents who were interested in helping within the music department, and I wanted to give them opportunities. I guess when I asked this teacher to supervise the show choir rehearsals, it threatened the other parents' perceived stake and control in the music department. I don't know if indeed that was the case in this situation, but I don't believe that anyone who genuinely wanted to help you as a teacher would ever speak to you in the manner in which I was on that message. It may be tough to tell, but beware of parents or anyone else who may want to help you as a new teacher because of ulterior motives. The only ones who should have control are you and your colleagues.

So, what happened? Well, unfortunately you have to keep dealing with people you don't like or who don't treat you fairly in every profession sometimes. Such was the case with me also. I saw the mother often in weeks following, but I decided not to confront her or call her back about the outrageous phone call, hoping that her outburst was merely a one-time blow-off of steam. How do you reason with that, anyway? As you will read later, however, my principal and this woman did indeed have a little chat. These parents didn't give up their active role in the music department, they didn't move to Antarctica and they never apologized; however another incident like this one has never happened since. And that, my friends, is fine with me.

November 28

Better day than yesterday—not sure
what I would've done if it was worse. I felt
like I got a lot accomplished today and that
always makes me feel good. I got the program
started for the Christmas Concert and did
some emailing. Jazz had a good rehearsal
and Fundamentals was a productive class. It
was a long day though, with revue rehearsal
right after school til 8 p.m., so that just felt
like forever. Because of the long day, I brought
my dog with me to school today. "J" stayed
in my office and behaved the whole day,
putting a smile on my face whenever I saw
him. Extra kids showed up for rehearsal to
do the light and sound board for the show
this weekend, so it was nice to have them
around.

November 29

Another busy and productive A day.
Getting the Band signed up and excited for
the fundraiser Christmas Breakfast. Chorus
way ahead of where we were in preparing
for the Fall Concert—we already have one
song pretty comfortable, so that's great.
Revue Rehearsal getting better and better—
actually I was practically giddy at the
rehearsal tonight...maybe it's because I'm
just beyond exhausted. I know it was not
because the mom from the other day's

phone call was in attendance and observing rehearsal. It made me feel really uncomfortable, like she didn't trust me. Dr. V. told me this mother came in to see her today about something else, and afterwards Dr. V. had a really stern talk with her defending me and how she will not stand for her teachers to be treated like she had me. I was relieved she did that—I don't have to stand alone.

I would like to take this opportunity to really impress upon you the importance of supportive administrators. They are worth their weight in gold. As a new teacher in need of knowledge and reassurance, your principal and other administrators should be your best resources. Don't be afraid to ask for their input, advice, or assistance. Don't be worried they will see you as weak or stupid. Your principal should be as willing to help you as they are to help a student...and if they are not, it is a serious problem. I have several colleagues who taught at schools where their principals or administration in general were not supportive or helpful; it was very hard on them, especially as young teachers. In fact, I had one fellow teacher whose principal did not stand behind her when parents called and complained about her grading scale: he overrode her grade and gave the student a better one without even being familiar with this student's performance in class. Now, I can't tell you what to do if you are in this type of situation, except to think seriously about the consequences if you were to sit back and do nothing. Conversely, if you are fortunate like I am to have a wonderful principal and fabulous administration, take the opportunity to thank them. Dr. V. — Thank you.

November 30

T-minus one day til the revue. The dress rehearsal tonight was productive and we received good comments from the couple teachers who watched and critiqued. I feel so many different things about it—on one hand, I get more and more excited about it and on the other, I'm sick of the kids, the long hours, and the stress, and I can't wait for it to be done. I made the spontaneous decision to have sectionals in Jazz Band today—I was walking up to the chalkboard to write down the order of rehearsal I had in my lesson plan and realized that I couldn't handle doing a rehearsal with them with everything else going on. I think that it was a productive decision because we got a lot ironed out, and it was timed well with three rehearsals left til the Christmas concert.

As I'm writing this, I'm supervising study hall with all kinds of thoughts running through my head. How many times have I been frustrated with teaching already this year? Everyone says your first year is always the worst and of course, I didn't believe it. I thought I would be different. How long have I spent wanting to be a music teacher...since sophomore year of high school it was...and now that it's here sometimes I wish I was back in college or doing something else! Sometimes I'm happy, but I wonder if this is the happiest I can be...or is there more out there? Teaching is this giving, noble profession, so I feel good that I am "making a difference" or trying to anyway, but sometimes I just want to be selfish and do things to make more money or for my personal ease of living. Is that so bad? But then I always feel bad for wanting that. All I was ever told in college was how inspiring teaching was and how enlightened I would be....Maybe that's not what I was always told—maybe that's what I always heard. Most days are not enlightening and that is disappointing for me. Does that make me a bad teacher? I have all these thoughts and I wonder if I'm having them because I am doing something wrong....

I'm sorry that we are leaving November on such a bad note, so to speak. I cannot guarantee that you will experience these same feelings I did...well, yes I can. The truth is that there are low points as a teacher, as there are in any profession. You just never plan on them. I never remember seeing my high school band director down or depressed, although now I realize that he couldn't have been happy all the time. My college professors never suggested that I might have to deal with issues like control-freak parents, negligent bus companies or my own self-doubts (if yours did, bless them). Every frame of reference pouring into my head of every teacher I ever wanted to be like was happy and serene. I thought that I was a failure because I had to be perfect, smiling, and pleased every day, and I wasn't. Here I am, a college graduate, a teacher, ready to take on the world, and isn't everything gonna be great, I thought. My life was not the fantasy I had set up for myself, and I was a fool to think it would be. There is nothing wrong with having high expectations and setting goals for yourself, but we have to learn not to crash so hard when we are stressed, tired, or when things just don't go well. There are lows in everything in life: relationships, finances, romances, and even (gasp!) sports teams. Your career is no exception. Your passion for education is stronger than a few bad days.

In order to get yourself through it, think about all the great things you've accomplished so far this year; don't focus on the negative. Approach a close friend or co-worker and be honest: tell them you feel down in the dumps and they will more than likely remind you how awesome you are...compliments are always a boost. Talk with some of your favorite students about their life outside of school— have a normal conversation with them. Treat yourself:

get some ice cream or take a bubble bath. Reinforce what a remarkable person you are. And look ahead to all the substantial things that you still have to attain this school year, what a fabulous job you will do, and how much you will continue to grow and learn.

December

December will fly by. You will be busier than ever. A major part of your life this month, as you would expect, is holiday performances. As the concerts approach, you wonder how it will ever come together. But when you work hard, stay organized, and put your mind to it, it all will. And your sense of pride and accomplishment is incredible…or maybe it's just relief. I know that's how my first December of my teaching career started: with a heaving sigh of relief.

> December 1
>
> A Friday of successful rehearsals with the Chorus and the Band, but the Strings I'm a little worried about. With the Christmas Concert coming up, some of them really have to buckle down and practice more. I gave the Show Choir a break—we signed thank you cards for our tech people and got mentally ready for the revue tonight and tomorrow night.

My reflection after the two performances of the musical revue:

> The revue this weekend was a success. The crowds did not fill the auditorium, did

not even come close, so I was a little upset about that. All of our effort...to not have the reward of sharing it with more people was disheartening, at least for me. Guess that next time we will have to do more advertising and promoting for the shows. But the kids displayed a lot of energy, clean diction, and some great dancing, showing that our hours of rehearsal were indeed valuable. The tech crew also did a great job with sound and spotlights. It was a new and fun experience for me to be backstage during a production, wearing a headset, watching the action on stage from that perspective. It was great to talk to the performers as they came off stage or help to pump them up before they went on. But overall, I'm really glad that it's over. The biggest surprise was the flowers I received on Friday before the show. They were from the family who, less than a week ago, left the voice mail that made me cry. I guess sometimes you never really know what to expect.

December 4

Good Monday—Jazz had a good rehearsal. We were practicing little things like accents and small phrases, then putting them together into the big picture of the chart, which worked well. Effective structure and sequence.

> I got a start on the programs for the
> Christmas Concert on Sunday. Being ahead
> of the game always makes me feel better
> and more in control.

The extreme importance of *sequencing* cannot be stressed enough. As music teachers, we feel that our rehearsal time always flies by so fast, we try to cram in as many concepts as we can, then hope and pray that students will pick them all up. Most of the time, that doesn't work. By starting instead with something smaller and easier (like one note or phrase as I did in the above jazz rehearsal) and building upon that, students will not only remember more...they will learn more. And they will learn it better. What is more effective or desirable: merely "getting through" an entire piece of music and having to re-teach it all the next class, or rehearsing and learning 16 bars really well?

> Interesting student situations today. The
> school held a prayer service during the school
> day. When I returned to my room afterwards,
> I found a bunch of students hiding in the
> percussion room. I told them that skipping a
> prayer service was a pretty disgraceful
> thing to do...then I turned them all in to the
> Assistant Principal. After school, I was running

errands up to the office and around school.
To continue the festivities, when I came
back downstairs, I found a male and female
student lying on top of each other, kissing in
the middle of the music room floor! Yikes! I
told them that their behavior was not appropriate for school, so they, umm, separated.
I guess it could've been worse, but I can't
believe that I deal with this stuff sometimes.

December 5

I'm still very busy with the Christmas
Concert approaching. I finished the programs for the concert and hung posters up
around school to advertise our performance.
Got some helpful fine-tuning done in both
trumpet and saxophone sectionals today.
The full rehearsal for Band was good also; I
feel they will do really well at the concert.
Chorus doing surprisingly well, too. I am still
concerned about the String Ensemble and I
am trying desperately to keep the Show
Choir focused. They were so lethargic today.
I think they are probably just really burnt
out from the revue, but they still have to
prepare a piece for the Christmas Concert.
We did have an insightful conversation eval-
uating the show, so that was worthwhile.

It is very important for students to learn to critique their work in any class or situation. In order to prepare students for the adult world, they should learn to rely not only on an instructor, but to utilize the concepts of teamwork, self-awareness, and personal responsibility for their success or failure. Musical performance is an especially beneficial genre in which to use self and peer-assessment because of its subjective nature. Obviously there is no denying wrong notes, rhythms, etc., but I am also referring to the emotional, expressive side of music. The crescendo that one person loved another might think was ineffective. The balance of a chord that sounded fine to the performers might have come across to a listener as being flat. This kind of open communication and evaluation is crucial in the development of an ensemble.

As I mentioned before, I did evaluations with other ensembles after our fall concerts as well. While the exact format may change, the general idea is always the same. I focus on two major ideas: critiquing the past performance and how that relates to our future performances. I also require the students to go beyond the simple reporting of facts to the examination of their feelings.

With certain smaller groups, the following questions could work well in an open discussion. However, I would suggest doing them in a private worksheet form for the most beneficial result for a larger group of students. To focus on the most recent performance,

I often merely ask what they liked about it as a whole, as well as what they thought about their own individual performance. So far, so good.

Then I get a little more personal, asking what they can improve on; specifically what they can do to become a better musician. What are their goals for the rest of the year? This helps them reflect on where they are as a vocalist or instrumentalist at the present moment, and where they want to go from that point.

I then inquire about how music and performing make them feel or if they feel connected to music or their fellow musicians. Questions like these are important because they stress the significance of emotional involvement in music. I think oftentimes these types of questions also remind students why they are musicians…and make them feel pretty darn good about it, too. For a sample copy of a performance evaluation, please see the reference section.

December 6

Continuing concert prep. Jazz Band doing well—starting to play tighter and coming together on rhythms. There were several very cool moments today where everything was just really clicking and I could see on the kids' faces that they could feel it, too. Started to hand out pit orchestra parts for our musical at the end of February…made kids happy I chose them, so that in turn made me feel good. Fundamentals was tough today. Some days in there are so good and others are so bad—there's such a difference in interest and maturity among the students. I don't want to give up on some of them, but I have to teach the ones that want to learn. It's hard to teach kids who have bad attitudes, talk all the time, or simply don't seem to care.

December 7

Today I'm completely spent. Practically constant rehearsals or sectionals all day, plus a combined rehearsal over lunch periods to work on the band, string, and choir finale piece for the Christmas concert. By Show Choir, which is close to the end of the day, the kids noticed how stressed out I was—it was pretty funny how they said I needed to eat lunch and relax. I felt that the day was productive though, and most musicians seem to be in good shape for Sunday. Plus, I'll be doing my part with the band kids and their parents at the uniform fundraiser Christmas Breakfast this Saturday. So it'll be another full weekend with school activities. Even though I was so tired by the end of the day I could barely think, it felt good to have everything coming together.

It's pretty common for us crazy music directors to put ourselves through this kind of sick torture in preparation for a big performance. However, there is a difference between wanting to put on a dynamite show and giving yourself a heart attack. Work hard, help your students to strive for their best, and then chill out. If you are a basket case, your kids will be too.

December 10 – Sunday – Christmas Concert

My first concert with all the ensembles combined, so it was a bit nerve-wracking, to say the least. Most of the kids did a pretty good job of getting to the auditorium on time so we could do a quick dress rehearsal: telling everyone where to go and when to go there, etc. They really listened, so organizationally, the concert went very well. No bad transition times, so I liked that. Seven groups performed roughly two pieces each, plus we performed the finale piece at the end. The concert was about an hour and twenty minutes —perfect. Not too long or too short.

Musically the concert was well done also—most groups did fine, but I was disappointed with some things. I just don't know what to do with the Jazz Band trumpets. I've been challenging them with some upper range pieces, but I guess I will have to start limiting that because they can't handle it. This week, they seemed to have good

---

rehearsals, but at the concert, they just lost it. The Concert Choir surprised me in a good way—they were much better than in rehearsals. Why they can't put that effort into singing all the time is another question.

At last, it was time for the finale, a band/string/choral version of "Do You Hear What I Hear?" The various ensembles and I spent a lot of time rehearsing this separately, but not much putting it together as a 100+ member group. How would it turn out? Would we all stay together? I gave a smile to the group, then the big downbeat. I heard lush chords, clear lyrics and passionate music...it was incredible! At the end, we got a standing ovation! It felt great to be conducting that many musicians at one time and have everything come together the way it did. What a gift!

There is nothing more satisfying than the feeling you get after a successful concert. The applause from the crowd, the smiles and looks of pride from parents and performers alike, and the knowledge that your time, effort, and tears have indeed made a difference are powerful feelings. I still get chills when I think back to that day. What a privilege and blessing to be in charge of such a meaningful experience.

December 11

    SNOW DAY! What better time to have an unexpected day off than the day after a concert! Sleeping late, being lazy for a change, catching up on a book I'm reading...I loved every minute of it!

December 12 – Tuesday

    Did a lot of low-key things with the kids today, being our first rehearsals after a concert. We discussed the concert itself and events coming up, and filled out some performance evaluations. Gave members of the Jazz Band some individual practice time. I am getting the next pieces of music we will be working on ready for the groups: making sure we have enough copies, collecting old music, etc. Even though some teachers think that I'll be "coasting" now until after Christmas break, and I even jokingly say that sometimes, I still have to be preparing for things that are two or three months away.

December 13

    Because of the snow day, this was the first time I've seen my A day classes since the concert. Plus it was an in-service day, so

> classes started at 10 a.m. and were shortened
> to 20 minutes. But we had some great discus-
> sions about the concert, filled out evaluations,
> etc. Chorus especially had some great things
> to say, no negativity this time. I also had
> the ensembles' hand in some of their music
> and do other organizational things. The Band
> kids were really loud and talkative today—I
> think that it's still better than the beginning
> of the year, but now it just grates on my nerves
> so easily when someone is talking when I am.
> I probably should've been stricter at the
> beginning of the year.

The eleven words of death. Well, maybe that's a stretch. The eleven words that no new teacher ever plans on saying, but most always do: I should have been stricter at the beginning of the year. It's something that your college professors all told you:

"Be very strict when the school year starts."

"You can always loosen up, but it's difficult to become more strict."

"Don't even smile until Thanksgiving."

While the last comment may be a bit of an exaggeration, we have all heard advice like this. So why don't we follow these words of wisdom? Let's ask ourselves another question first. As new teachers, what do we want most? What have you found yourself hoping for with the most passion? A huge budget? No. A dynamite marching band? Maybe. For our students to like us?

Most assuredly. But wait...another thing we were all told was that it shouldn't matter if our students "like" us or not. Will the students "like" a strict instructor? How do we sort this all out?

First of all, I think we can all agree that needing your students to respect you as their teacher is crucial. But we cannot overlook the issue of wanting to be liked by our kids. Wanting to feel as though you are "liked" is a basic part of human nature. Who wants to make their living by teaching young people who don't like them? No one thrives if they feel unwanted or unappreciated. Additionally, I don't think that anyone can even feel truly successful if they don't feel liked. How satisfying is it if you have an award-winning choir, but don't feel the slightest bit admired by those students?

I know I wanted my students to like me as a first year teacher. I still want my students to like me, as a teacher and as a human being. But during my first year of teaching, too often I associated students liking me with being "likable." I wouldn't yell or discipline as much as I probably should have. I excused too many inappropriate behaviors. Eventually, as I became more comfortable in my teaching role, I wised up and was downright sick of the things I earlier had let slide, such as talking while I was talking, not paying attention or not keeping the music room clean. You may think it will get better by itself or you may think that it's not a big deal...but it won't and it is. While I was wondering what was wrong with my kids, my kids were surely wondering why I was changing.

Being liked isn't about being nice every second of the school day. In fact, if you are easy-going all the time, your students may not take you seriously. Eventually, this leads to a chain of events where your students don't feel you take the music program seriously; then they won't either. The end result will be exactly what you were trying to avoid...your students won't like or respect you or your program.

So, how do you balance being caring, friendly, and likable with the right amount of strictness and control? Think back to the music directors whom you admire. The qualities they probably displayed were dedication, knowledge, passion, discipline, and enthusiasm, just to name a few. Did they inspire you by not yelling at you when you deserved it? Did they invigorate you by being nice all the time? More than likely, they pushed you to succeed and transferred their love of music to you by emphasizing hard work and getting in your face every once in a while. The teachers whom students "like" are the ones who help them be their best: the ones who care enough to be jerks sometimes.

It was tough at first to become stricter, but I'm glad I did. The kids looked at me a little cross-eyed for a while, but eventually they realized that I was serious...that I wasn't giving up on improving their musical technique, rehearsal etiquette, manners, or cleaning habits. It gets a little bit "old" sometimes to stop rehearsal because of behavior problems. I get sick of repeating "Be quiet, please," or, "Put your stands in the rack before you leave," all the time, but in the long run, it's worth it. It is definitely better than ignoring the problems and wishing they would solve themselves. Little by little, the whole classroom atmosphere becomes more efficient and successful as the result of just a little more discipline and structure.

So follow that advice from your professors or co-workers about being strict at the beginning of the school year. Find the right balance of discipline, humor, caring, and musicianship for you and your group. Think long and hard about the rules you will set in place and enforce them from the first minute of class to the last. It may not be easy, but your students will not only like you for it, but they'll respect you for it, too.

Sometimes, though, ya just gotta let loose...read on....

December 15

Allowing two girls in my study hall to have a handstand contest for the last five minutes of the hour (I don't know why they wanted to so badly—they begged and begged), as well as other things made today an obvious Friday. I decided to do bonding games in Chorus, like name games and the "human knot" game (see reference section for ideas). I felt they needed to be a closer-knit group, so that was my plan to try and make that happen. And surprisingly, fifty kids doing activities around the entire music room was more under control than I thought. Good sight-reading in Strings and Band sectionals, and the Band did well with rehearsing pep band music for the basketball game tonight. The game itself was fun—the team lost, but the band played well and seemed to have a good time. Tonight was the first game we played for, so I have to get used to the routine of playing during time-outs, etc.

I am still mad at the Show Choir for not returning all of the scripts and music books from the revue. No one seems to know where the missing books are. I have to send it back to the company a.s.a.p. or else we may lose our security deposit. Next time, I should number the books in pencil and write down the people they correspond to so I know whose book has been turned in. I feel completely incompetent screwing that up.

While they may be high school students and technically "young adults," they still need a guiding hand with that "responsibility stuff." Additionally, middle school and elementary students aren't too young to experiment with some responsibility concerning objects and property. They should be capable of keeping track of music, folders, or books to some extent. But by numbering those items, making announcements or reminders, or giving kids secure places to store these items, we can help them along and set them up to succeed.

December 18

Monday—beginning of last week before Christmas break. Trying to take it easy, yet not waste time, and give kids a solid basis for their (hopeful) practice over the break. I gave Chamber Music Ensemble a practice day to work specifically on their duets and trios, and sight-reading new music went well with Concert Choir and Jazz Band. I am really trying to be intelligent about the way I introduce pieces—trying to really get the kids to think and observe things.

Frustrated with the usual students in my Fundamentals class. I realize that a lot of the things I want them to learn are complex, like music theory, but their other classes are complex, too. The fact that a few of them don't even pretend to listen or try to understand is the most frustrating. I try to engage them the best I know how. I wish I had more time to prep for the class, but that doesn't give them the right not to listen or to not try. It is rewarding to help the other kids, but it feels like it's not enough—I want to get to every student.

It is like giving a gift and having it thrown back in your face. It is like preparing a fine feast only to have your family tell you they are not hungry. When students act as though they don't want to learn what you have to teach them, it is difficult not to take their attitude as a hurtful rejection, even though they probably don't realize their actions are creating that effect. As musicians, we are passionate about our art form and want everyone else to be also...sometimes that is just not the case.

One would think that students, especially high school age, are in music classes because they really want to be—because they feel that sense of enthusiasm about music that you do. Unfortunately, that is not always the story. Adam is in band because his parents bought that two thousand dollar saxophone, and by golly he's gonna get good use out of it. Avery takes choir because her friends did. Matt enrolls in music appreciation because he thought it would be an easy class. Soon it becomes apparent that the parents' wishes, the friends' social skills, and the class's imagined simplicity are not enough to make the child succeed, and problems arise.

So how do you deal with students who have different effort and achievement levels in the same class? How do you not let a few students drag the rest down? Unfortunately, there is not an easy answer to that dilemma. What I can offer is a few tips and ideas to help you come to some conclusions of your own.

First of all, as much as you may want to or as frustrated as you may be, you cannot ever give up on a difficult student. You may not believe it, but that student needs you more than you realize. A student who is doing poorly in your class probably has issues in other classes as well. His or her behavior and attitude problems are most likely not isolated. Students like these need your guidance and love, as tough as it may be. If you give up on them, like so many others probably did in the past, you add to their defeat. In their eyes, you continue their streak of rejection and worthlessness.

Don't count on these students to show you this defeat, however. Sometimes these students are, on the outside, the most confident, cocky, or sassy young men and women you know. Don't let that fool you. Think of ways to break through that phony exterior and get to the core of their being. Only there can you really start to teach and help these challenging students.

Some things I tried and had some success with are as varied as the students themselves. One big concept that worked well for me is spending time individually with students. Often in a classroom setting, students feel threatened or want to show off in front of their peers. Incorporate one-on-one lessons, tutoring or teacher/student conferences into your curriculum. In this setting, you remove many distractions and help the student focus more on learning. Secondly, give students choices and let them have some extent of control over their education. Independent projects are a great way to achieve this, as they give students the opportunity to learn about something they want to know more about. For example, in my Fundamentals of Music class, I allowed the students to choose their quarter project topics, with the only guideline being their subject had to relate to music in some form. This really fostered their creativity and gave the entire class the opportunity to learn about many different topics, from Irish music to John Williams to carpel tunnel syndrome. More importantly, these kids with whom I normally would struggle to get excited about anything were *eager* to learn and wanted to excel. I would call that a success.

December 19

So I graduated from college a year ago today...and here I am sitting in a study hall observing bored, apathetic looks on young faces. It's kinda depressing. I guess I don't know what I expected life to be like, though. Everything seems so different than just a year ago. I was so naïve—just ready to go and be successful and happy. To be honest, I thought I was ready for anything and I would be the best teacher anyone ever saw. Right now, that seems pretty far off the mark. When most of my time is taken up telling kids to be quiet, taking attendance, doing grades, etc. rather than making music, it's difficult. How much of a difference am I making? Am I teaching anybody anything? Am I a failure because some days I don't want to be a teacher? Why do I deal with kids who talk all through Chorus, then bitch because they want to pick out better music? Why do I have percussionists who don't respect property or equipment? I guess I thought that I could come into my first teaching job and kids would automatically act the way I wanted them to...that problems happened to other first-year teachers in other schools...I think that I just need Christmas break to arrive...fast!

With the above mental conflicts jumbling up my head, I was asked to put together a "mini-Christmas concert" assembly in two days as a "nice send-off" on the last day of school before break. Mind you, our actual concert was over a week ago and all the music was handed in and probably dismissed from the students' memories by now. The last thing I was counting on before break was a practically impromptu concert in front of the entire faculty and student body.

So, while the rest of the teaching world was giving tests, presenting projects, and basically winding down before the Christmas break, I was as stressed as ever, handing out music...again, and rehearsing holiday musical pieces...again. In a way, it was more stressful for me than the formal concert because it was in front of both the kids' peers and my colleagues.

While my principal commented that the performance did not have to be anything fancy, it was still very important to me. I felt as though my reputation was on the line, that students and staff would be judging me and the quality of the music department. As families, friends, and community members usually attend our formal concerts more often than teachers and other students, this would really be the first time they would see me in action. I really wanted to show off the kids' efforts as well as my own, and put on a great performance.

In addition, it was difficult to organize this assembly. I had no idea where to begin and neither did any other teachers because this type of holiday program was never done before. Looking on the bright side, no one could really compare what would be my fumbling efforts to anything previous. Besides organizing things like risers, chairs, and stands, trying to manage 200 kids was a project in itself. Setting up equipment and trying to get them to listen to directions in a gymnasium when it was two hours until Christmas break was a tough job for one person. Combine this frustration with my nervousness and desire for perfection and I wondered if we would even remember the right notes to sing or play.

As the student body and staff started filing into the gym, I felt another wave of anxiety. Why were these 16-year olds making me nervous? Suddenly it hit me: I felt as though I had something to prove. Not only as a new teacher, but also as the leader of the music department. At my school, like in many others, music is not seen as the absolute "coolest" thing to be involved in. I felt like I had a duty, a responsibility as "the queen of the geeks" to show that music at our school was great.

Despite all of the crazy factors surrounding us, the students played and sang beautifully. I spoke intelligently to the audience. They seemed to listen attentively. For barely being able to contain my anxiety, things ended up running like clockwork. I received many compliments from other teachers at the luncheon afterwards, so that felt good. At one point during the concert when the Chorus was to come from their place on the bleachers to the stage area, I simply gestured to them and they all immediately rose to their feet and took their places. One teacher commented on that action and said that she wished she had that kind of presence and command. I have to admit, it felt great, but I think that nine hundred pairs of eyes were probably a part of that, too.

The downside to the event was that some of the students did not do as good of a job cleaning up as they should have. After the faculty Christmas luncheon concluded in the cafeteria, I got stuck making several trips from the gym to the music room, taking down music stands, chairs, and percussion equipment all by myself. I was pretty ticked about that. They perform well, now I just have to teach them responsibility. I shared that comment with some of the other teachers; they laughed and said I was asking a lot.

Should it really be that impossible?

With that thought, we leave December. We leave the month as we began it: with a heaving sigh of pride, accomplishment, and relief. Enjoy your successes, have a wonderful winter break, and come back reinvigorated and ready to continue meeting the challenge of music education. It will be a new year with many possibilities.

January

The month of endings and beginnings. You are beginning a new year, but ending the first semester. Larger projects like giving semester finals and calculating budgets for next school year are looming, as are smaller, fine tuning lessons and concepts you are anxious to teach students, now that they have four months of school under their belts. You are leaving holiday lessons and performances behind and starting new music for contests and spring programs. You may feel like you know your students well by this point, or, more than likely, you still encounter surprises. By the time the month is over, the school year will be more than half-complete...you are either breathing a sigh of relief, or saying, "But I still have so much I want to teach them!" Crazy things will still occur, but are you learning from your past experiences and dealing with things more effectively? I'm not sure I was...but I was trying.

January 3

First day back after vacation—actually, I felt ready to come back and start tackling new projects like Large Group Festival and the spring musical, "Fiddler on the Roof." Purposely planned some "laid-back," review rehearsals to ease kids back into the swing

---

of things. After school, one of my String
Ensemble students gave me an update on her
personal life—I always like students talking
with me like that. Got a bunch of new work
to do in the administrative department, such
as the budget for the department next year.
How am I going to do it? This year isn't even
over, so I don't know what I'll use or need as
far as on a yearly basis, but I'll figure it out.
Also have to plan what I'm doing for semester
finals in all of my classes.

Doing a music department budget for the first
time was a tough and stressful task. It was something
I worked on long and hard, but I still don't think I
did the best job. As a first year teacher with no other
colleagues in the department, what sort of frame of
reference did I have on what was really needed or
how much money I really had to request for those things?

My advice for you is to really take time in doing
your budget—don't rush through it merely to get it
off your mind. Think seriously and thoroughly about
the needs in all of your classes: the things you use
every day, as well as the things that may only come
up once a year. Allocating money for new music,
drum heads, or office supplies is often a given, but
don't forget about things like piano tuning, instrument repairs or replacements, festival fees, bussing
costs, uniform dry-cleaning, or music department
awards and plaques. If possible, request a copy of

the budget from last year to use as a guide. Lastly, don't be shy! Ask for as much as you feel is necessary to run a quality music department. It may not all be approved, but your administration cannot consider what they don't know about.

January 4

   I felt a little out of sorts this morning and I'm not sure why, unless my sub-conscious was hinting at what was going to happen later in the day. I began telling students about their various final exams and everyone took it well until I got to the Show Choir. They jumped on me like a pack of wolves. They began saying how they never had a final before in this class, why was I doing it, etc. What they were saying didn't bother me nearly as much as their attitudes did and how they were saying it.
   "WHAT? We're having a FINAL?"
   "Like we don't do enough! That's SO unfair!"
   "This is SO stupid!"
   "SIGH!" (followed by shoulders slumping and eyes rolling)
   I never experienced such bratty behavior as I did at that moment, and I didn't know how to handle it. I literally froze and began stumbling over my words because I was so taken aback. I halted the conversation and said I had to reflect on what just happened, so I would talk to them about it next class.

Maybe I have given them too much control or too many choices and they have abused that freedom. I don't know, but I was very upset about the way they talked to me and treated me.

Later, I went to talk to Dr. V. about it and she said, as the co-director of the musical, which has recently started rehearsals, she was experiencing some attitude problems from the very same students! So in a way, it was a relief to know that it wasn't just me. I am going to have a serious discussion with them—me talking, them listening—and I think I am going to write myself notes outlining exactly what I want to say. I've never had to do that before with any of my groups when I've wanted to tell them something, but this is a special circumstance. I really want to say everything right.

Tomorrow is one of my best friend's birthdays. She is also a music teacher—specifically a middle school band director. I took her out for dinner tonight and we discussed the various ups and downs of teaching. It was nice for both of us to be able to tell our feelings to someone who really understands.

I cannot stress enough how important it is to socialize with other music teachers. Hopefully in your school, in the actual building or in the system, there is another music teacher whom you can bounce ideas off of, scream your frustrations at, or just simply talk with. We music educators have our own set of glories and challenges, as do math, science, foreign language, or physical education instructors. Teachers as friends and peers in other disciplines are obviously great, but be sure to have several musical contacts as well. That way, when you are frustrated with those trumpets who can't ever hit that high C, you will know who to talk to for sympathy and suggestions (fellow music teacher) instead of receiving a dumbfounded look (rest of teacher's lounge).

January 5

Nice that it is the end of the week already—even though it was a short week it sure had its highs and lows. After getting some hints from Dr. V., I wrote some notes to myself in preparation for the Concert Choir. Since some of the same kids are in Concert Choir that gave me such a difficult time yesterday in Show Choir, I wanted to be prepared and I didn't want to wait until Monday to address the problem. So I felt bad that I was lecturing some kids who, in a sense, were "innocent," but I hope that it was educational and preventative at least.

Please enjoy the following ideas from my "speech" to the choir students:

"I have to share with you how disappointed and hurt I was by your poor attitudes and negative body language yesterday. The presumption that you would not have a final before you even spoke with me was wrong. It makes me feel as though you are "blowing off" this class.

"I take the policies of this school and the requirements of my job as a teacher very seriously. However, I am also not merely 'following the rules,' but doing what I know is right. The purpose of a final is not just to give you all one more thing to do or another hoop to jump through; I am giving you a final to help you become better musicians. I care about your education, musical knowledge, and growth. I wanted to assess you in a way that will not only show how you have grown through this semester, but also help us continue into next semester. Why are you in choir if you don't want to better yourself as a vocalist?"

"Band, String Ensemble, Chorus, Fundamentals of Music—all of my classes are having some sort of semester final. It is my right as a teacher to assess my students. Not one of these other groups whined when I informed them of their finals. What kind of image does that depict of your ensemble? What kind of opinion might that give the rest of the music department about you? Is that the attitude you want to portray?"

"Some of you made the comment, 'We've never had a final in this class before.' My challenge to you is: be accepting of change. This is a new school year, I am a new teacher and you are a new, different person than you were last year. Think about the changes that your parents and other adults have to accept every day in their workplaces, within their families, and in their general communities. Many of you make the comment that you want to be treated as young adults…in order to be treated in that manner, you must begin to act in that manner. Take your responsibilities seriously in every part of your life and try to embrace change instead of fighting it. I think you will find that your life will be happier and more serene instead of stressful and antagonizing."

"So, even though I've strayed a bit from the topic of your final, I feel that the thoughts I've shared with you today are important life lessons and I hope at least a few ideas 'struck a chord' with you, so to speak. The answer is, yes I am giving you a final; however, to avoid conflicts with other finals which are scheduled at the same time, your final will be on our last class day before the finals schedule starts. I have put thought into this and feel that this is an appropriate compromise…now, please, any questions or comments?"

The students were struck fairly silent and seemed okay with what I had to say—I didn't get the crappy attitudes or sour faces, so that was definitely better. In fact, many had their heads bowed and would hardly look at me—was that from defiance or embarrassment? In the end, I received some apologies and agreement about the test arrangement. I was very nervous about having this kind of "talk" with them, but I'm glad I did it. I tried to not "scold" them necessarily, even though I was upset, but to inspire as well. Maybe some of them will remember something I said and it will help them live a better life...isn't that the bottom line of what teaching really is? I can only hope.

On the up side to this week, the Jazz Band had great rehearsals, so that's been awesome! They are really continuing to make progress, not just as an ensemble, but I am hearing substantial individual improvements as well. It puts me in such a great mood when groups make progress like that. Played pep band again for a basketball game tonight and it was fun—big crowd there and the kids played well.

January 8 and 10

Took Tuesday the 9th as a "sick day" to spend with my sister (ssshhh). She was visiting me from out of town and leaves for Scotland for a semester of study abroad next week. It was a nice break, but when I got back on Wednesday I found out barely any of my classes met—kids had study halls instead. That made me upset. But I was also happy: the kids all said how much "it sucks" when I'm not at school because they can't hang out in the music room, so that kinda made me feel good.

> Anyway, Monday and Wednesday went pretty well—good rehearsals, reviewing for their performance finals, etc. Had the first pit orchestra rehearsal for "Fiddler" Wednesday after school and it was rough. I'm glad the first one is over (I'm also glad the school hired a vocal director for the musical—I couldn't imagine trying to be in charge of both the orchestra and the vocal parts! Since the musical is considered an extra-curricular event, all rehearsals will take place outside of the school day. I will not conduct any "Fiddler" rehearsals during class; the choirs and instrumental kids involved in the musical will continue working on our other music during the school day). Not many of the instrumentalists have played in a pit before, so the style, counting, etc. is tough for them to get used to. Wednesday night was also the first of two registration nights for incoming freshmen next fall. I enjoyed it—it was fun to help new parents and students and to sell them on the music program.

Again, a good example of recruiting and how it can help your music department is illustrated in the above journal entry. Just like with open house, take your responsibilities at freshmen registration, or any new student registration very seriously. Parents accompanying their first child into the unknown realm of high school will be there; be gentle and understanding. Students unsure about signing up for a music class will ask you many questions; be informative and enthusiastic. Think of ways to attract positive attention and bring parents and students over to your table to talk with you. Have the video of the holiday concert playing or display some pictures of your students. Be inviting and be interested in the prospective students' lives, not only their future at your school, but also what they are interested in currently. Let them know how special they are. Their fears and insecurities will melt away and hopefully they will flock into your music department.

January 11 - Thursday

Because my lesson plans didn't get carried out when I was gone on Tuesday, this is the only day my B day classes are meeting this week—not the way I wanted it, but I'll deal with it. I am beginning to doubt the Concert Choirs' ability to sing the Brahms' "How Lovely is Thy Dwelling Place." It is on the "Class A" list and it is difficult, but I thought they were ready for it. A comment was made way back from this group that "if the music you gave us was harder, we would pay more attention." I was happy to oblige, but so far that hasn't happened. Interesting when you call students' bluffs and the promises they make fall apart.

I also met with two uniform salesman today—it was very irritating, informative, and all kinds of other things at the same time. Mainly, I realized how much money it's

---

going to take to get new Marching Band uniforms, even more than I was counting on.

January 12

Last A day, besides finals days, of the first semester—in a way, it's tough to believe that the year is half over. I wonder if this past semester or the coming one will be more difficult. Fair rehearsals today for a Friday—Band was a little goofy and didn't remember a passage in "Moorside March" that we drilled a lot last class, so that was a little frustrating. Just glad that I planned to rehearse it again today. Also not happy with their memories on the "Amazing Grace." That will be our required piece for large group festival, so it has to be great. I can't figure out the String Ensemble—most of the 2nd Violins are doing great on their short solos I just recently assigned them, but other things they've had for a while, they can't play even as a unison section. Weird. It'll be interesting to hear them play individually for their final next week. Most of the Show Choir did fine on their individual singing finals...and didn't grumble. It was definitely helpful for me to see who knows the music well.

As far as the String Ensemble is concerned, the more I thought about the above phenomenon, the more it made sense to me. At the time, we were rehearsing Handel's "Entrance of the Queen of Sheba." In this particular arrangement, there are many short four-measure solos in both the first and second violin parts. Instead of assigning all of the solos to the section leaders, I decided to make the educational experience equal for all and give every violinist in the ensemble at least one solo. When I think back, I remember how excited they were and how special and proud they felt. So they took home their own respective solo and must have practiced the daylights out of them; they sounded great in a very small amount of time. Why? Why would these parts in this particular piece come together faster and better than other music that we rehearsed for much longer? Simple. They felt important. At least for a short time, they knew it was up to them, and only them, to make the ensemble sound its best. Which is great.

However, it is also important to convey to any musical ensemble the necessity of doing their part for their entire section as well. Like I stated above, many violins in the String Ensemble could play their solo parts beautifully, but fumbled on their tutti sections. I think many musicians, no matter what their age of experience, often feel that in a group, their individual sound is not important. They have thoughts like, "If I miss this note, who will know the difference?" or, "Someone else will cover that rhythm" or my personal favorite, "Maybe that tuning problem will just go away."

How do we as music educators help solve this problem? I have found the *recording* of rehearsals and performances extremely effective. In an ensemble setting, it is often difficult for musicians to step outside of themselves and listen to the whole picture. And your word as a director may only go so far; the kids want concrete proof. To use the String Ensemble as an example once again, I told them again and again about a chord that was out of tune. We tried many things to resolve the issue, such as taking the notes out of context, singing the pitches, etc. But whenever we put the ensemble back together and started the section again, the same problem came back. However, when the group heard the *recording* of the section, they really noticed what I was trying to say. The same holds true with any group; a jazz band that has muddy articulations or a choir that displays poor balance or blend. Recording that sound and playing it for your students often proves to be a useful tool in getting your musicians to hear what you do and want to make it better. Every part, from second violin to fourth trombone, is important, and we as teachers must be sure every student knows that.

January 15 – Monday

　　Last day before finals for the first
semester. The A day schedule is used for
finals, so I did finals with my B day classes
today. Listened to the Concert Choir and
Jazz Band in small sectionals for their semester
final—both went well. I think that many
things were both solidified and cleared up,
especially with the rhythm section in Jazz.
That's what finals were for, so glad that
they were productive.
　　"Fiddler" rehearsal better than the first
one—know that each one of the kids will get
more used to the feel of "musical music" as
we put more rehearsal time in. It's really
neat to work with a lot of the "top" musicians in the school since they are so talented
and serious about doing good work. They
sight-read and adjust quickly. But it does
make for a long day with a two-hour rehearsal
tagged onto the end of the school day.

Tuesday, Wednesday, and Thursday, January
16th through the 18th, was my first experience
with a semester finals schedule. Each day had three
ninety-minute periods, ten minute breaks in
between and ended at noon. In general, they were
good days for me; the fact that the days were shorter
made a difference, as well as it being a break from
the everyday pattern.

> On Tuesday, I had one final and it was during the middle period of the schedule (I let myself sleep in a little bit, which felt wonderful). My final for the day was listening to small groups of about four Chorus students sing the music we've been working on. They did a good job, but I myself can never time things correctly. I ended up getting through all of the groups with a lot of extra time left in the testing period, so I could have tested them in even smaller groups.

During the next test period, I had a meeting with the principal and two of the Advancement office personnel about the middle school solo contest that is held at our school every year for middle school students. At first, I was nervous and apprehensive about it because it seemed like a lot of work to organize. No one seemed to know anything about how it was done in the past to help give me a frame of reference. As the meeting went on, however, my fears diminished. We talked through the planning of the event and it sounds like it will be manageable, as well as a good tool to recruit young musicians to our school. I actually became excited about the project—before I thought about it as just another thing to take up my time. I was glad that I kept an open mind…good advice for teachers in any new situation.

> Wednesday was my big day for finals as I had things scheduled during all three final periods today: String Ensemble individual playing tests, Concert Band sectional tests, and Fundamentals of Music project presentations. I liked the schedule of the day, but it was very mentally draining. I was an active observer for all three finals—not at all like giving a traditional test. Four solid hours of constantly paying attention was tiring, but I was glad I did them because the students played well, and the performance-based exams are worthwhile and relevant in my classes. Day topped off by a two-hour pit rehearsal.

You may be thinking, why wouldn't one use that time—ninety minutes uninterrupted—to conduct an in-depth rehearsal? Most directors certainly feel as though they have limited rehearsal time, so an opportunity like this was tempting. The idea crossed my mind more than once. However, think back to the objective of a final: how do you as a teacher want to assess your students? How do you want to hold them accountable for their success or failure, their "A" or "F?" When I thought about the situation in that light, I knew I had to do something different than holding just another rehearsal. Besides, in a typical rehearsal setting, your students may be merely repeating the same errors. In a smaller performance test environment, musicians know the heat is on.

You will be tuned in only to them and will hear every clash of a wrong note or blip of an incorrect rhythm. This in turn (hopefully) motivates them to practice even more than usual, since they won't be able to "hide" within the section or ensemble, and ultimately moves the group further along than an average rehearsal would have. At least that is what happened for me. Maybe you will have a different experience, but I would suggest giving playing tests a try. In fact, I wish I could do more of them, but frankly, I don't have enough rehearsal time.

> On Thursday of the finals schedule, I didn't have any finals to give and that was fine with me. It really could have been a day off for me, but I felt that it would be unprofessional if I didn't at least come in and do some work for part of the morning. I got my grades done, practiced saxophone (my principle instrument), did some emailing, etc. Tomorrow is a "real" day off, a small break between the semesters, so I will definitely enjoy that.

> January 22
>
> Monday and first day of the second semester—it almost felt like a miniature first day of school. Lots of students were goofy and not focused. My schedule really doesn't change except for the times of the

study halls I supervise—all of my classes run all year long. Concert Band had a good rehearsal today; they played "Amazing Grace" a lot more beautifully than they have in recent past. Maybe those playing tests at finals time really helped.

Started to teach the Show Choir more of the difficult rhythms in the "Bill Bailey" piece they are doing. It was rewarding because some of the time, I feel like a lot of them are much more advanced singers than I am...and I think they have that attitude, too. So in a way, when they don't know something, I feel good because I can help them—is that twisted? Like I want them not to be good at something, like counting rhythms, so I can help them and feel like a better teacher? I don't know, but it was nice to start them on that challenge and help them figure out the complex swing rhythms.

After the school day was done, my actual day was only half over. Another pit rehearsal—it gets better every time, but it still is a slower process than I thought it would be. We need to start getting through the music more quickly because we haven't even touched the music in Act Two yet. Then, after a way-too-short time at home, later tonight was a Band Parents' Meeting with the uniform rep. It was so long, like almost three hours, but it went well and people are definitely excited about getting new uniforms! Tomorrow morning the rep will stop into school again and we will draw up a sketch

> for a sample! Apparently we have to get
> moving, because in order to get the uniforms
> by August, we should order them soon.

The above mess is a good example of having *too many things going on at once.* Oftentimes, one of the hardest things about my first year of teaching was not the teaching part, but the "extra" things like parent meetings and uniform decisions. I never dreamed that during my first year as a music director I would be designing new uniforms for a marching band! Not only that, but I never imagined that these "extras" would consume so much of my time. Having rehearsals for the spring musical as well as playing at pep band engagements during this time of the year did not help either. I found myself extremely tired, ragged, and stressed out.

If you are finding yourself in this same situation, take heart. Music teachers in general have a lot on their plates, but as a young or first-year teacher, you have even more to digest. My advice to you is simple...do your *best.* That is all anyone can ask of you. You cannot become superhuman, deprive yourself of eating or sleeping, or drive yourself crazy in pursuit of "perfection"...there is no such thing. Not only that, it is not healthy and such behavior will backfire in the long run. I think many teachers spend countless hours giving their all, then hours more worrying if their work is good enough. Don't put yourself through that. Obviously, we all want our labor to bear sweet fruits, but have faith that your efforts will prove successful. And if something does not go exactly as you planned, use the opportunity to learn from your mistakes. Lastly, always make time for yourself. As I stated before, if you are not happy and healthy, you will be of very little use to your students.

January 23

After a successful rehearsal on duets and trios in Chamber Music Ensemble this morning, the uniform guy came back and we discussed the sample uniform—hopefully will be able to see the actual fabric sample in a few weeks. It was exciting! It really feels good to be helping to build something like this at the school. Jazz Band is continuing to have great rehearsals, and today especially was really satisfying. We made a lot of progress on both of our pieces for solo and ensemble contest. It was great to hear music really come together with that group today. During Fundamentals of Music there was a speaker scheduled in the theatre making a presentation about the care of disabled people, so we attended it as a class and tied it into an essay and discussion on music therapy. It was a cool coincidence for that to be scheduled, so we could attend during our class time. I really felt like a quality teacher today.

January 24

   Very weird, stressful day—just one thing
after another that I wasn't ready for. My
keys got locked in my office—some students
were in there hanging out and shut the door
with the keys in there. Not a big deal, just
irritating. Then, either I missed the memo
or it just came right out of the blue, but
the yearbook decided to take pictures of all
"groups" in the school today, music, sports
teams, etc. The endeavor interrupted String
Ensemble and my sectional schedule, and I
ended up having to help organize all of the
kids. Again, not the biggest deal, but it was
something that I hadn't planned for. Maybe
I need to get better at dealing with these
unexpected things.
   Thin crowd at pit rehearsal today after
school, but it's going okay—most songs are
learned as much as possible until we join the
cast. Sometimes I am just so exhausted by
the end of the day.

Read on....

January 26 – Friday

   There was a pep rally for the hockey
team today and it was a disaster for the
Band. I was so mad that I don't think I

cooled down until about two hours afterwards. The only time the pep rally committee wanted the Band to play was during this quiz game they were playing with some athletes—we were supposed to be "background music." Well, of course we were too loud for that and some snotty seniors that were sitting by us started harassing us. I really bitched them out, but it probably didn't do any good— sometimes Seniors think they are the gods of the earth. It was really tough to see the pom squad do their routine and be showcased, but not the Band. It broke my heart to see it hurt a lot of my kids.

So I marched right up to the pep rally committee (a couple of teachers and students) after the rally was over to voice my concerns. I had to let it out right away. They were very understanding, so hopefully we can all work for the next pep rally to be more "band friendly."

Tonight, the Pep Band played at the hockey game and it really made up for what happened during the school day. The parents were very appreciative that we were there and the kids enjoyed a different atmosphere from the basketball games. Made me feel better.

There is no question that you should stand up for your students and the music program, but be very careful *how* you defend your students or voice an opinion. As angry and frustrated as I was in the above situation, I never blamed anybody for what happened, nor did I raise my voice or act unprofessionally at any time. As much as my temper was trying to get the best of me, I didn't allow it. Surely you are in this business because you are passionate about your students and their music. Don't let that passion get the best of you. Do not make enemies out of the very people whose support you most need—that of your own faculty and student body.

I'm glad I spoke with the pep rally committee and began to work more closely with them because the pep rallies to come were much more successful, at least from a band point of view. The band had more opportunities to be featured just as much as any other student group, and I could tell my kids were happier. However, I don't think it would have happened that way if I would've gotten too bent out of shape about the above pep rally. Keeping your cool produces results.

January 30

Today is Tuesday—we had another snow day yesterday. Even though it was nice and I used it to sleep until almost noon, the results today were not that great. Kids were giddy from having an unexpected three-day weekend. They were inattentive and passed around pictures from the weekend's T.W.I.R.P. dance (The Woman Is Required to Pay—I

---

had to ask, too). Again, A days with giving sectional lessons, supervising a study hall at the beginning of the day, teaching straight through from 7:30 – 1:00 is really straining. Everything just happens right in a row and it's hard to focus on the very different classes. It's not like it's four sections of the same Freshmen English class, it's a study hall, Chorus, String Ensemble, Concert Band sectionals, Full Concert Band, and Show Choir. Most of these classes couldn't be any more different from each other.

I'm also tired of the lack of participation and poor attitudes from a few people in the Band who decide to forget their instruments all the time or do homework behind their music stands. I reprimand them and they don't seem to care. It hurts my feelings more than I thought it would. It makes me really frustrated and I wonder why they don't care. I know I am not a patient person. I know with hard work the program will grow and change with time, but what else can I do to keep helping it along?

January 31

Today was a really bad day for me. Nothing super bad happened, I was just in a mood and felt totally depressed and down. Maybe it was just a culmination of the past few days, but I cried on my boyfriend's shoulder practically all night because I felt so bad. I just don't feel like I'm doing a good job sometimes. I didn't expect teaching to be so hard and take so much of my energy. Is it because it's my first year? Is it because of all the different classes I teach, so it'll be better next year? Or am I really not cut out for this? I have a hard time just "getting through" the first year until another teacher is hired—that's not my style. I want to do the best job I can and be great all the time. Which I know is somewhat unrealistic, but that doesn't mean that I don't still feel bad. And I'm still not doing well with being so tired all the time. Teaching just sucks the energy out of me. I want to be a great teacher whom kids like and respect and remember and learn things from and are happy about it...but at what cost?

One thing I was not prepared for when I entered into the teaching profession was the absolute emotional roller coaster it can be sometimes. During the past week of journal entries, one day was great, the next was not. One day, everything clicked and came together, the next was scattered. I am sure that by this time in the year, you have noticed this as well. Please know that the feeling is universal—it happens in all schools, to all teachers of all subjects. We are human beings, and we work with other human beings. Mistakes happen and emotions overwhelm us sometimes. Breathe. It's okay. What is not okay is for us to wallow in our disappointments. Sulk, comfort yourself, then get back in the game. Try to appreciate human nature, not condemn it. Celebrate your good days more often and don't put so much stock in your bad days. Believe me, I know that is much easier said than done. If nothing else, take comfort in the fact that someone else knows what you are going through. In our careers, relationships, and all other facets of our lives, we are all "works in progress." Take pride in the work you have done so far. And if you have to, force yourself to relax for once.

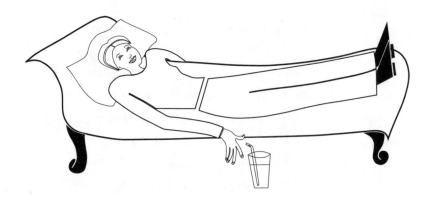

February

While February is the shortest month of the year, in "school time" it must surely be the longest. There are usually very few vacation days, projects seem plentiful, and large group festival performances abound. However, this is not entirely a bad thing. I feel I made some great progress with some of my performing groups this month. There were fewer breaks in the schedule and the knowledge of the upcoming, judged performances provided a challenge and motivation for many. This month also contained the majority of joys, heartaches, and just plain work concerning the spring musical. With our opening performance less than a month away, there was no time to waste....

February 1

New month—new vows. After my ups and downs last month, I'm pledging to be serious about music, but to try not take myself too seriously, to know that it's okay not to be perfect, and to try my best to give thanks for what I have and already do. I will stay positive. But I think I know how much work is coming up with "Fiddler" and Large Group Competitions and I'm already dreading it. I know that sounds bad—I know the product will be great in the end with hard work, but

> I don't want to think about how tired and
> stressed I'm going to be. I am just going to
> have to exhibit lots of energy, because the
> more I give, the more I will get back...I
> hope! Remembering to always keep trying.
>   Today was better than yesterday—I had
> a great moment during Concert Band when
> the kids were playing beautifully. I was con-
> ducting this wonderful music, thinking that
> this is what teaching music is all about – these
> moments are the ones to live for!

And the roller coaster continues! Make these happy fulfilling moments the cornerstone of your existence as an educator, instead of the low budgets or poor attitudes. Like I stated at the end of the previous chapter, it's okay to feel depressed sometimes. Just don't stay there. Make your own vows and remind yourself to live up to them every day. Have a plan; your workplace wellness is too important to leave vulnerable to the whims of everyday catastrophes. I think the old phrase, "Success is getting up one more time than you fall down" rings even truer when adding, "And while you're up, remember how crummy it feels to be down." Very few people ever actually *desire* to be down; however, it happens to all of us at one time or another. By taking an active role in our feelings and being aware of what we as teachers need to do to stay healthier and more serene in our professional lives, we will not have to "get up"...we'll already be there.

February 2

Friday of a long week—even with the "snow day" on Monday, this week seemed really long! Better Concert Choir rehearsal today...except for the fact that the basses can't sing. But we started a new section of a piece and they did pay attention—it's like I always have to be a couple steps ahead of them or something. They don't like polishing and reviewing music as much as learning new parts, which is hard for me to understand. Why wouldn't they want to sound not merely "okay," but great? I guess that it's both good and bad—I'm glad they like learning new things, but I need to figure out a way to make the concept of polishing and "making music" vs. "reading music" more appealing to them.

Jazz had a weird rehearsal today: it was good because they seemed to focus most of the time and we drilled a lot of complex rhythms, but bad in the fact that their memories were poor. Some of them kept forgetting things we did two minutes ago. Attitudes were flying around today, too—the saxes were criticizing the trumpets. Even though the saxes were right that the trumpets weren't doing the best job, the comments obviously were not the best way to solve the problem. I should've said that at the time, of course, in addition to my "teacher look," but I always think of the most intelligent things to say after the fact.

As musicians, I'm sure you know the vast difference between performing as an ensemble body alone versus accompanying a group of singers in the style of a musical theatre production. But it's often difficult to teach those concepts to high school kids who have barely even seen a musical, much less participated in one. Make sure that you address balance issues right from the first moment you join the cast, perhaps even before, so students will know what to expect. Balance in a musical does not only mean that the pit orchestra plays softly so the vocalists can be heard. It also means playing with a supported tone, blending and projecting, as well as playing louder and more pronounced when the pit orchestra has the obligatory "fill" at the end of a vocal phrase.

Another important issue to agree on is obviously tempo. When the pit orchestra joined the cast in my above journal entry, there were many songs where the singers and the instrumentalists were at very different speeds. There were many points during rehearsals where I had to stop the cast and pit orchestra altogether, clap or sing a tempo, and really make them focus on one another. Encourage flexibility among all parties and work to achieve the most musically effective product.

Adding onto that concept, actors, directors, pit orchestra members—everyone involved in a musical production works hard and may get defensive or huffy at times. (Try and tell the lead soprano she is taking the tempo too slow, informing the first trumpet he is out of tune, or suggesting to the choreographer that she is being consistently forgetful). They may think their way is the only way to accomplish a goal. As I stated before, take it upon yourself to be a steadying, guiding, understanding force. Try to ignore or eliminate unnecessary arguments and get your students to do the same. Focus on the goals—the production and the well-being of its members...and everything else will take care of itself.

> The rest of the school day was fine also—I had the Chorus listen to parts of the "Schindler's List" CD because of the movie medley we are singing. The very next period, I got the brainstorm to use it in String Ensemble just for fun. We are not playing anything in that style currently, but they enjoyed listening to the orchestral sections. They thought that I was giving them a break, but little did they know my true intent....

The use of *models* in the classroom is so important, especially in a musical setting. You can talk about what a good concert band, an excellent choir, or a superb string ensemble sounds like until you are blue in the face and still your students may not understand. Utilizing a model to demonstrate, whether live or recorded, will drive the message home much more effectively. Think of all the possibilities: a student could be a model by playing or singing a particular line in a piece. Recordings on compact discs, cassettes, videos, or even dusting off the good ol' vinyls have the potential to be great learning and modeling resources. Maybe a guest performer from a local symphony would be honored to do a clinic at your school. Even you could perform for your class...when was the last time you played your horn or sang for your students? I bet they would love you for it.

February 6

Today I was in the school's music library picking out some new music for the Concert Band. We are doing well on the pieces we have right now and will need others to begin after Large Group Festival. Then I really starting thinking even more about the current work we're doing—it's kinda tough—I mean, our pieces sound great, but can we make them sound even better? Are we reaching our full potential? Am I helping their progress?

What is "the top?" How do we measure student musicianship and performance? What is "good music?" What is "better?"

I don't have an answer to these serious questions. What I believe, however, is that these are important questions for us as teachers, and perhaps more crucial for our students to ask. Why should the music director always make the decisions about what sounds good?

By asking our students if they like what they hear, we engage them more fully in the rehearsal process. Instead of merely following our orders for fuller dynamics, better diction, or more accurate tuning, they use higher level critical-thinking skills, such as analysis and evaluation. Students have ears too, and distinguishing ones at that. My guess is that most of them want to sound just as great as you want them to sound. Don't underestimate their potential for this type of assignment.

Here are a few ideas for executing this effectively. One thing that I would not do is randomly ask a group how they think a certain piece is going. Unless you have a really mature group of students, you are bound to get several answers you probably weren't looking for; consequently, the concentration level in the room may fall dramatically. A more successful approach may be to select a few students from the ensemble whom you trust to sit in front of the group during rehearsal. Design a worksheet for them to fill out to positively critique what they hear.

Have the entire group participate in this exercise by recording the ensemble and playing it back for them to analyze. I discussed using this idea post-performance, but these techniques are also tremendously effective during the process of learning and rehearsing a piece as well. By getting students out of their own parts and listening to the group as a whole, they perceive more accurately what needs to be done to help the ensemble perform even better. On many occasions, I had students exclaim, "Oh, so *that's* what the melody sounds like!" or, "Wow, that chord *does* sound really bad." Making music should be more than following a director's instructions; it is most fulfilling when discoveries are made, both about the music and about ourselves. Please refer again to the reference section for the sample performance analysis worksheet.

February 7

Long day with "Fiddler" after school—was more frustrating than the first rehearsal on Monday, so I was admittedly crabby toward the end. It is very difficult to put a pit orchestra together with vocalists. Between the singers changing tempo all the time and some of the pit not knowing their parts as well as they should...it's a mess. Plus Dr. V and Mr. A, the co-directors of the musical, are getting on my nerves. I know they want the production to be wonderful and I know they want the kids in the pit to practice more. But it seems to me they have other problems to worry about, like singers not knowing their pitches or actors forgetting their lines. Instead, they spent the end of rehearsal giving the pit orchestra a 'talk' about practicing their parts. I know we need to get better, but it feels like they are making us a "scapegoat" for the musical not coming together. We still have over two weeks, and we've only rehearsed with the cast three times. I appreciate their concern, but I feel like they are looking down on me or taking over my job—I'm the orchestra director, not them! I just wish they'd have faith in us. They're talking about bringing in outside musicians and I am totally against that—it's a high school production, not Broadway. I know that everything will fall together in the end. It's my first production in a director role—I'm still learning, too.

If I had only known what was to come next week....

February 9

Today was my first formal observation by the principal, Dr. V. She sat in during concert band, watched rehearsal and took notes. I was a little nervous—I know that we have a good working relationship, so I wasn't scared or anything. Rehearsal was pretty good, too—her presence helped most kids' attention spans and we got a lot of work done. (Too bad she can't sit in all the time!) But I was nowhere near prepared for the conversation we had after the observation. It was great—better than I could've ever possibly hoped!

She loved the way I ran rehearsal, how I balanced friendliness with being business-like, and how I conveyed my love for music and the ability of trying to transfer that to the students. The notes she wrote about my observation were very inspirational to me and made me feel successful, which is so helpful, especially when I'm not feeling that way myself. We talked about other things, like how I feel about being tired, lonely, etc. sometimes. It was nice to talk to someone about that and to know that it's normal. I still want to push myself to do better, but it's good to know that someone thinks I'm on the right track.

It also felt good to make Dr. V feel good—she said that she got a lump in her throat watching me conduct because it was so beautiful! It felt great when she said it made her day to watch and help a beginning teacher.

My next experience deals with both my professional and personal lives. My boyfriend and I got engaged during this second weekend in February, which was obviously amazing and wonderful. I was never so happy in my life...or so distracted. Here I am in the midst of the busiest time of the school year so far, trying to manage the musical and large group festival, not to mention upcoming solo and ensemble performances and just plain teaching every day! It was a great time in my life, but also a very stressful one. Many of you as young teachers may encounter the same thing: you graduate from college, secure a job...then that right person may come along with whom you want to spend the rest of your life. You may not think that it will affect your work, but it will. Which is not a bad thing, however just be aware of this and have a plan for managing your time and energy in this regard.

February 12

Monday—very hard to come back after my weekend-long vacation with my new fiancé! It was so wonderful and it went so fast—I think back on it now and seems as though the weekend happened in the blink of an eye! But the day was fun personally for me to show off my ring and telling everyone about being proposed to!

Getting down to the wire with Large Group Festival—it is two Saturdays away, which ends up to be about five rehearsals. Of course it is happening one of the same

weekends that "Fiddler" is running. The Concert
Band is going to be fine, but I am worried
about the Concert Choir. It's tough because
so many of them are in the musical and they
are concentrating their efforts there.

The show itself is coming together.
Tonight, we ran the entire thing and it's
obviously still rocky, but the progress is
there. The directors are still being pretty
hard on the pit. I know they feel that the
pit is bringing the show down, but I wish
they would let me deal with it. There are
many other aspects of the show that are
far from perfect that I think they should
spend their energies worrying about.

February 14

Well it didn't feel like Valentine's Day,
that's for sure. Nobody's "feeling the love"
for me right now. I feel out of the loop,
unimportant, and out of control. Today I
found out that Mr. A, one of the directors
of the musical, went and hired some college
trumpet player to "help" in the pit orchestra
without asking me. He asked briefly about
this idea last week and I said that the kids
would practice more (which they did), and
we'd give them a few more days. I thought
the pit was sounding a whole lot better, but
what do I know? Obviously not as much as

> this history teacher who is doubling as a
> musical director. So it was never finalized
> with me. Do you know when I found out
> about it? Do you care to guess? At the
> beginning of rehearsal when this poor col-
> lege kid walked in and Mr. A introduced us.
> So there I was, standing in front of my kids,
> and I just wanted to explode. I wanted to
> scream and defend myself, my students, and
> our work.

But I didn't. I took my burden and suffered in silence. But all was already spoken—by the eyes, the body, and the heart. My students looked at me with countless emotions in their faces: confusion, anger, despair, concern. They knew. My pain was theirs. They felt the same way I did...the director just violated our respect, our dignity, and our musicianship.

Why didn't I speak up? Why didn't I tell the director how I felt? The truth is I didn't know what to do. But I do know how I felt. First of all, I felt intimidated. I was a 24-year old female first-year teacher up against a 50-yearold male veteran teacher with an overbearing "Type A" personality. As confidently as I know my convictions and methods, it all escaped me when I was put "on the spot" and told this strange, non-student was joining the pit orchestra. Secondly, I felt angry. Thoughts were sprinting through my head at a pace I couldn't control, so I knew that my third, more forced emotions of self-restraint and coolness had to shine through. I thought of my kids, my dedicated 16-year old musicians who sat in front of me, no doubt hanging by a thread, waiting to hear my response to this unwelcome news. So I chose to be calm and accepting—a catcher bringing another wild pitch under control. I calmly introduced the college musician to the rest of the group and tried to be as friendly as possible: the situation obviously was not this young man's fault. What kind of role model would I have been if I got carried away with my feelings or acted unprofessionally?

But I also wanted to show my students how to stand up for themselves. I wanted to enlighten them about being passionate about what they believe is right and just. I wanted to guide them in possessing grace and professionalism in the face of adversity. I found myself wanting to teach my students more than one life lesson that day, but discovered sometimes, that is impossible. How could I have been passionate, angry, professional, and demanding all at the same time? To this day, I don't really know if I did the right thing, if I made the best choice. But what is "right" or "best?" What was the main idea I wanted to come from that situation? I hope that my students did not see me as a coward that day. Instead, my hope is they saw me as a mature, capable, understanding human being.

I also have some comments about the professional and musical ramifications of these circumstances. As a young or new teacher, I hope you do not have your credibility challenged like I did. It felt horribly demeaning, and for a teacher who is trying to establish respect and competency among students and other teachers alike, it seemed like I was ushered several steps backward that day. Please don't do what I did and suffer in silence. You may have to if it occurs in front of students, but my advice is to find that person later and discuss how their actions made you feel. I never did that in my situation, and to this day I harbor unhealthy feelings toward this drama director. How much more sense it would have made to bring these dialogues out into the light and clear up failures and misunderstandings! The director, in his quest to make the production the best he could, probably didn't even realize how his actions impacted me or the pit orchestra students. Even though you may feel uneasy or intimidated, try to talk things out in these situations.

Be forewarned, however, that even with the best intentions, you may not end up with the results you hoped. The other party may have such a vastly different philosophy than you, it could be difficult to see eye to eye. In my case, rightly or wrongly, I was extremely against adding adult or outside musicians to the pit orchestra. I know it is a common practice: "musical" music is quite difficult and often not best represented by the instrumentation of a high school music department. Nevertheless, I firmly believe a school production should stay just that—a school production. Sure, you may not get the professional quality product, but what is your first responsibility? Some of the students we teach will never have these kinds of opportunities again after high school, so it is our primary duty as educators to be exactly that—educators for children, not community theatre directors looking for praise or a perfect performance. The experience we give the kids in our school should always be the first priority. And if a student is not accomplishing something, it is our job to help and guide them, not to replace them.

February 15

A local university band director came to do a clinic with the Concert Band today. I think it was beneficial and the kids really enjoyed it—he was great with them. It helped them to see a different conductor and work on techniques in a new way. Plus, it was neat for me that he came early, so the two of us had almost an hour to talk. I don't have the opportunity to talk to a fellow music professional very often, so it was very helpful for me to have somebody who really understands and can put things into perspective...especially with everything going on lately.

The "Fiddler" trumpet issue came to a head this morning in Dr. V's office. I requested a meeting to discuss it with her and Mr. A. Last night at rehearsal, the college trumpet player told me that Mr. A. said he wanted him to play the first trumpet part. My student had been practicing that book for almost two months, now Mr. A. wanted my student to start playing new music? One week before the open of the show? I couldn't allow myself to be left on the outside of these decisions any longer, so I walked into Dr. V's office with a fire lit under me.

The outcome could've been worse. The college guy is apparently in the show no matter what I say. But I would not budge on the fact that my student will play the first part and this college kid will be a support person, mainly playing the second part and doubling the first part on higher notes if necessary. They were agreeable to this compromise, which was a relief. I'd given in too much already and feel like my credibility had been shattered. It was really tough to face the two of them by myself, but I'm glad I stood up for what I wanted and what I thought was right. I don't need this stress! I really can't figure out why this is such a big issue—the directors seemingly aren't upset about actors who don't know their lines or singers who don't know their pitches, but the fact that the pit orchestra trumpets are fracking a few notes is cause for major alarm. Plus I feel so sick—bad cold and sore throat, but I'm trying to hang in there.

It was very difficult for me to face my principal in what I thought was such a defiant manner. As I have stated many times, she is a wonderful person and was incredibly supportive of me during my first year as an educator. But this was the first time I had not seen eye to eye with her on an issue, and I was very uncomfortable in doing so. I thought that by disagreeing with her, I was negating everything she had done for me...that I was being a spoiled brat.

Remember that you will not always agree with everybody, even someone whom you consider to be a mentor figure to you. It doesn't make either one of you a bad person; it just means you have different ideas about how to accomplish something. Don't be apprehensive about sharing your feelings and opinions in a respectful, positive way. Someone who really cares about you as a professional and as a person should listen and agree to a compromise.

February 16

Today I stayed home sick for the school day, but came in for "Fiddler" rehearsal after school...is that crazy? Are my priorities of education skewed? I'm not sure....

February 19 - Monday

Well, tech week for the musical is here. Today's rehearsal was the first full run of the show with full make-up, costumes, everything.

I thought it went fairly well—hopefully this week will be a lot easier than last week. Everything is coming together and sounding good...the question is...is it worth the cost? The musical has been very draining on a lot of people and has given me and many others a lot of stress and unnecessary hard feelings. I wish I had more to write about than the musical, but it truly is all-consuming. I know that it will be satisfying in the end to hear the audience laugh and applaud, and to know that we accomplished something wonderful. Maybe the looking back and remembering will be fonder than the actual experience itself.

February 21

Concert Band had a really great final rehearsal today before the Large Group Competition this Saturday. I feel like they will really do a good job. String Ensemble, on the other hand, has not had very good rehearsals lately. The second Violins are just stagnating—I know they are trying to get better, but it's such a slow process. They need like ten minutes on every single phrase. Next year, I'm going to try to schedule the Strings over the lunch hour so we can practice in sectionals during home-room time like the Concert Band does.

Dress rehearsal for the show tonight contained a few big stressors right off the bat. The "talented, older, wiser" college trumpet player who Mr. A brought in, who skipped rehearsal the last three days, finally showed up again and was totally screwing up...I say fine, let Mr. A see how stupid he was for bringing in this guy. Plus, a student violin player who hadn't rehearsed with the pit for like two weeks because she had been "sick" graced us with her presence, too (mind you, this is a girl who is absent because she's "sick" almost more than she's in school). I gave her permission to play because I really didn't know what to say, but during the run I realized that it wasn't happening for her— she was completely lost most of the time. Even though she said she'd practiced, it just wasn't falling together and a lot of the other players were upset. I can understand why— they have put in a lot of time and work and now this person, a peer, just walks in and wants to be allowed the same honor of playing. Not to mention that her mistakes were messing everyone else up! I don't know what to do. What is a good option that is fair to everyone and doesn't discriminate against the girl for being sick?

One of the hardest things for me about teaching is having to be the "meanie" sometimes, especially in a situation like the one above. How do I deny a student the opportunity of participating in a huge school event because she says she was sick, no matter what my gut really says about her absence? (In this situation, I think this girl really was not sick. I do not mean to be unfeeling, but she was rarely in school at any time of the year, not just this month. She never made up homework in any of her classes. She always came back to school with a different excuse: her friend died, she was in the hospital, etc. and these stories were never documented). But in the same breath, how can I allow all of my other dedicated musicians' work to be compromised? One of my philosophies of education is that everyone should be treated equally and have access to the same opportunities. However, I realized that what the individual students decide to do with those choices and equalities are up to them, and those decisions may have consequences they don't particularly like.

February 22

Dr. V. and I met with the truant violin player this morning and told her she couldn't be in the pit. It was tough, but it was something we had to do. She seemed very disappointed, yet she also seemed to understand. We tried to make it clear we were not trying to "punish" her for being "sick," that sometimes things are just not meant to be. This whole musical has just been one project or crisis after another—things that I never thought I would have to deal with.

Concert Choir had their last rehearsal before Large Group Festival today, and I think they will get a two rating. They're just not focused or prepared enough to get a one with this contest being the same weekend as the musical, even though the contest perform-ance is during the day and the musical is at night. I almost wish I wouldn't have entered them because they really don't seem to care. Yet they have these huge attitudes and think they're the best choir ever—I don't get it.

Jazz Band continues to have good rehearsals—they perform at the Solo and Ensemble Festival next weekend. I was also much happier with Fundamentals class today. First of all, I buckled myself down and somehow found some time to prepare more thoroughly. The kids seemed ready to listen today and I assigned what I think will be worthwhile homework: everyone in class is taking a section of the Baroque music history chapter to read and report on to the class. Then the other class members will critique, take notes, and ask questions for each presenter.

Never underestimate the power of preparation!

As far as the choir was concerned, it was an interesting phenomenon. Many of their egos were flying high on an individual basis because of the musical, and that aura transferred into their classroom setting. Obviously, it is a great thing to have confi-dence, but these kids thought they were invincible. Even though they hadn't put nearly the effort into the contest preparation as they had the musical, they didn't seem worried about walking off with the highest rating.

I think an effective way to educate kids in these situations is to take them to a music festival or contest where they have the opportunity to hear other musical groups. Festivals like the one we were going to attend are usually held at a school. There are generally three judges who listen to the group and critique their performance, both orally and with written comment sheets, which the group receives afterwards along with a rating. You are not competing against anyone; therefore, any number of ensembles can be awarded a first rating. Firsts are for a superior performance, seconds are good, thirds are fair...and down from there. Not only do the students benefit from qualified judges studying their performance, but they also learn from listening to other groups. Besides the field trip that previous autumn, the choirs never heard other student groups their own age and ability level. Don't get me wrong, the Concert Choir was pretty good, but there were many things they could have done much better that I don't think they ever wanted to realize or admit. The festival demonstrated that quite well....

February 24 – Saturday – Large Group Festival

Freezing rain and bad roads made for an interesting bus trip into the city for Large

Group Music Festival. Also, I had to deal with the irritation of "special privileges" for the leads in the musical—they didn't have to ride the bus with everyone else, they got permission from my "favorite" drama director to sleep in and drive themselves later in the morning. Is that fair and reasonable or not? All I know is that I was disgusted by it, and maybe that gut reaction is the right one.

Anyway, the Concert Band performed first and played practically the best I had ever heard them! I was so proud! It felt so good! The judges' comments were more than I could have possibly hoped for, like "I'm struggling to find some things to improve on." One of the comment sheets had "well taught" written on it, so I was thrilled! One judge stood up after we performed, introduced himself, and shook my hand; that made me feel special as well. What a great experience for me and I hope for my students as well.

The Concert Choir, to be honest, was tough to care about. They didn't make a good effort, so it was hard for me to. I try my best, but sometimes it's just exhausting. They performed okay, but could've done a lot better. After our performance, one judge came forward to give his comments...and they were plentiful, abounding in constructive criticism. Inside, I rejoiced because it was so refreshing for them to hear comments like that from someone beside myself. About how yes, there are things they can do

better. Maybe it's cold of me to feel this
way, but I'm glad they were "knocked down a
few pegs." The deal was particularly well-sealed
when we listened to the Choir who performed
after us—were they ever awesome! I could
see the doubt, amazement, and awe on their
faces. Especially after that final blow, they
probably didn't think that the Festival was a
good experience, but I did. I hope it will make
them think about things they haven't before.

In case you are curious, the choir did receive a
second rating. The concert band got a first.

As far as the opening weekend of "Fiddler on
the Roof" performances, they were definitely experiences to remember. Opening night itself was really
exciting! There were so many emotions swirling
around the music room as the pit orchestra students,
dressed to the nines in their black performance
wear, were warming up: anticipation, exhilaration,
nervousness, exhaustion—all were very present,
like a bittersweet aroma hanging in the air. We had
been through so much together: long days and nights
of rehearsal, hurt feelings and unfairness, the stress
of wanting to do a phenomenal job yet balancing the
rest of our lives and our sanity, and in the end, remembering why we were all there in the first place. I felt
it was my place to try and bring everything together
for all of us.

About ten minutes before we were to go upstairs

and take our places in the pit for opening night, I asked my students to join hands for a prayer. I said a few quiet words of gratitude—for the opportunity, the music, and the presence of every student there. After a moment of silence, I asked others to share their thoughts and prayers, and many students had moving words of thanks and inspiration. Then in celebration, I opened the bottle of sparkling juice (the closest I could legally get to champagne), and we all toasted to a great run of the show. It was important to me to set a tone of celebration and success for the next two weekends of performances. I wanted to show them my feelings of gratitude and appreciation for their hard work and to reward them not at the end of the show, but for the journey of getting to this point. Those short moments were so touching for me as a teacher that I can honestly say it made all of the hardships I went through worthwhile. In the end, touching those students' hearts was really what the musical was all about.

That weekend, we had three great runs—Friday and Saturday night and Sunday afternoon performances. Saturday night, my fiancé and a friend of mine came, so that show meant the most to me personally; however, it was probably the worst performance of the three...it figures. Sunday was definitely our best show. In short, with performances of the musical and the local music festival, it was quite a weekend! When you are this busy, Monday comes around again awfully quick.

February 26

It was fun today to share the Large
Group Festival comments with the Concert
Band. I wish they would've been more attentive while I was talking—here I am, basically
telling them how great they are, and they
can't even pay attention for that! Because
of that, I don't think that I complimented
them as much as they deserved, but they
really have come a long way. I will try to
keep reinforcing that throughout the remainder
of the year. I did give them the rest of the
period for free time today as a reward for
their efforts.
Tonight was another long band parent
meeting, seeing the sample uniform, discussing
fundraiser options, etc. So much for a night
off! With the musical and everything else
going on, I've barely had any time to myself.
I feel like I've been living at school and it's
really catching up with me. I was very
cranky with my fiancé tonight—finally, I
just broke down and started bawling
because I am so tired and overloaded.

I think now is a good time to address burnout.
Not whether it happens or not, because it will happen at some time to all of us, but that *it is okay*.
There were many times during the school year
when I felt burnt out and overwhelmed. Not only
did I have those feelings, but I also felt bad on top of

that because I had those feelings in the first place! I felt awful for feeling burnt out because I thought if I was doing a good job, I wouldn't feel that way. I thought if I was truly enjoying teaching, these feelings would not be an issue. The fact that I couldn't justify *why* I was experiencing these emotions of exhaustion and inadequacy made me feel even worse.

It's important to note that burnout is not necessarily the same thing as being depressed or sad. For example, the above journal entries were part of a fairly happy and successful time during my first year of teaching. I was not "down" or doubtful of myself or my abilities during this time—I experienced many successes through performances of the musical and school music festivals. However, along with these accomplishments, there was the nagging physical and emotional weariness that wouldn't go away, no matter how successful or proud I felt.

The same thing may happen to you and my advice is to let yourself accept the feelings of burnout. Do not beat yourself up for feeling run down, especially after several high-stress events, weekend activities, and/or sixteen-hour days. Being burnt out does not make you a bad teacher; on the contrary, it probably is a sign that you have been working above and beyond what is required of you toward the betterment of our younger generation— surely a sign of a dedicated, good teacher.

But that knowledge in itself probably doesn't help you feel better, so here are some tips to help you in healing those feelings of burnout. On days that are particularly stressful for you, make it a priority to carve out some time, no matter how short, just for yourself. Those of you who have families might find this extremely difficult, but you must try—even a ten-minute period will help. I addressed some of these same issues back during your interview process, as well as when life was getting crazy in November, but a reminder is always helpful. At this time of the year, de-stressing is just as important, if not more so, than before. Use this time to do something that, 1) you enjoy, and 2) will help you relax and take your mind away from school activities. Some things that work well for me are taking a brisk walk, soaking in a bubble bath, reading (a novel, not lesson plans), closing my eyes and doing a brief meditation, or playing with my dog. Again, allow me to stress how important it is to not feel guilty about being burnt-out or having to take time for yourself. You must care for yourself so you may in turn care about your students.

February 27

Boy, was I tired this morning! Personal life things—my apartment is full of boxes since my fiancé and I bought a house (wow!), so we are getting ready to move. I didn't get home til 9:45 last night because of that meeting, then back at school early again today. It's just a lot to handle right now. Then while I'm here doing my job, I have to deal with Concert Choir kids who feel they are either too good for everyone because they're in the musical or they're too tired to participate in class. I want to say, you know, I'm tired too, but I'm here doing my job. Is that the difference between children and adults? It must be one of them.

Anyway, it's amazing how much the Jazz Band either retains or doesn't retain from rehearsal to rehearsal, especially like today's when there was a weekend in between. After last week's rehearsals, I really felt like we were ready for Solo and Ensemble Festival this coming weekend, but today things were sloppy and out of focus. I think we will recover and be fine, just as long as they can concentrate enough to remember what we've worked on. Fundamentals was great today—the format I chose of individual students reading and reporting on certain sections, then doing worksheets together, worked well. The kids really paid attention and seemed on-task. I always have a good feeling after that class when it has been productive.

And so it is with mixed feelings that we end February. As in every month, I had so many experiences I never dreamed I would have; I learned so many things. One of the most valuable concepts I realized about my teaching was the necessity of being human.

Many times, we think we have to be controlling, perfect, twenty-four hour role models who never have a bad day or show emotion. Not only does this set us up for failure, but it also isn't fair to our students. After all of my very human, emotional experiences, especially this month with the musical, I realized that the option of trying to be perfect and collected all the time was, in fact, not an option at all. This is not a license to slack, not care, have low standards, or be an emotional wreck; on the contrary, by admitting you are human, prone to making mistakes, and needing to display feelings, you free yourself to become a more authentic teacher. You will be happier and more at peace, too.

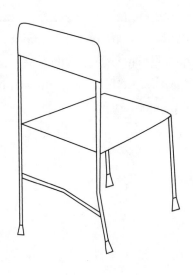

March

To me, March is another balancing act. It is like a see-saw, with one end lifting students toward the end of the school year and the other keeping them weighed in the reality of the moment. The third quarter ends, but there is still one more to go. Solo and ensemble competitions and spring concerts are fast approaching; however, big productions, like the musical and large group festival, are wrapping up. The long-awaited "spring break" is on the horizon. Some students, especially Seniors, seem to begin "coasting," dragging their feet, hoping to glide with ease through the next three months, while you as their instructor fight feverishly for their continued effort and faith in making great music. Which is often very difficult, especially considering what I dealt with on the very first day of March....

March 1

"Ms. B. is a bitch." You would think these words would affect me when I saw them, written on a chair in the music rehearsal room. It definitely surprised me, but I'm not as upset as I would expect from me, knowing my sensitive nature. I was more disturbed about the property being damaged. I felt a leap in my stomach when I saw it, but it did-n't take over my thoughts for the rest of the day. Is that because I'm so tired I can hardly see straight? Is my reaction just numbed? Or is it just something that I'm secure enough to look beyond, realizing my accomplishments and being proud of those instead of being torn down? But do those matter if this is the image I portray? Is it an overall image or the thoughts of one student? What do I do with the desk? Do I try to find out who did it; do I go broader and give all my classes a "respect property" lecture?

Why don't I know what to do? Why weren't things like this talked about in college? What did I do to make someone not only think, but write that anyway? When I told my fiancé about it, he said it sounds like I'm doing my job and being a good teacher. I'm making the kids work hard and some of them proba-bly don't like that. Perhaps that is true, but is it more than that? I care about them, how they sound, and what they learn—does this individual who wrote this stupid thing not care? Sigh, I guess it does bother me more than I first let on...not to the point of obsession, but to the point that I feel powerless and full of questions.

Well, that was not my favorite experience of the year, that's for sure. But I was proud of myself for the way I handled it. First of all, by simply writing my feelings in my journal, I felt better because I was able to give my questions and emotions a healthy outlet. It put things in perspective and made my thinking clearer. And it helped me remember an important concept. I once heard that in the field of teaching, it's important not to take things too personally: even if you get a desk thrown at you, don't take it personally. At first, I thought that statement was ludicrous. Personal attacks coming from young people whom I teach and care about are very hurtful—how can I not take them to heart?

Then I took a moment to recall my own adolescent life. I, like every other human being who goes through the phase, was full of confusing emotions, uncharted energies, and a thousand questions about who I was and what the world around me was about. I know I was angry with my teachers sometimes when I was in school, even my beloved high school band director, probably for no reason other than my mood at the time. Not enough to vandalize a desk over it…but perhaps I can understand these feelings, as well as students and their entire lives and feelings in general more fully by doing more reminiscing. It is very healthy because it helped me remember that students have their own separate lives and thoughts from me which I cannot control. I realized *I am not a bitch just because this one student happened to think so on this one occasion.* I am not justifying the action of the graffiti; I am acknowledging that it is okay for that student to feel that way. And that is a big step for me.

The second, physical part of the story was almost as educational as my emotional journey.

Needing to take action, I hoisted, heaved, and pushed the desk down to maintenance. Our head maintenance man who I'll call Rudy was very nice about the entire situation. Surely knowing how any teacher, much less a first-year teacher would feel, he chuckled and said, "So, someone's not happy with you, eh?" I grinned slightly and shrugged. He continued to advise me not to worry about it—I wasn't the only teacher who had ever had graffiti written about them. He carted the tainted desk into his shop, said he would take care of it and thanked me for bringing it to him. The exchange may not seem significant; maybe it simply relieved me to have the desk out of my sight. But I feel it was more than that. To have someone else know and understand and to have assistance in taking care of the problem…this counteracted a little more of my often-felt teacher's alienation and helped me remember that I was not alone. From the principal to the custodian, everyone has the potential to make a difference.

March 3 – Saturday –
Instrumental Solo and Ensemble

Some great learning experiences and some good opportunities for me to talk with parents and students and support them in a different environment. It was neat to experience solo and ensemble festival as a teacher instead of a performer—to let someone be nervous for a change! However, it wouldn't be normal for me not to go through a couple of fiascoes, so the Jazz Band was happy to oblige. Our bari sax player forgot his mouthpiece, so a guitarist drove him home to get it. Along with those two important players, a few other students showed up just as we were called to perform. But we got seated, took deep breaths to relax, and began our judged performance. Considering everything, we played okay—but we had much better rehearsals this past week. The judge had some good comments, but we ended up with a 2 rating.

Many other groups played at the festival today as well—several groups from my Chamber Music class performed duets, trios, and a combined ensemble piece. Several students also played their own solos to be judged. A few earned a "starred first" rating, sending them on to the state festival!

I cannot say enough good things about music festivals such as solo and ensemble contests. It is a lot like the large group festival the concert band and choir attended, only for soloists and smaller ensembles. Hopefully your state or district has some kind of opportunity like this for young musicians to showcase their talents. Not only is it a good learning experience for students to be critiqued by a judge, but students also feel a sense of pride and ownership by preparing music for a contest and working towards earning a rating. Festivals are usually held at an area school; they last an entire day and create an environment where music and music students are appreciated and celebrated. Many of you probably participated in music festivals like this while you were in school. Now, as a music teacher, be as supportive and helpful as you can to aid your students in being exposed to the same rewarding event.

March 4 –
Sunday – closing night of the musical

Tonight was the last of four shows for this weekend, Thursday through Sunday, and the last of all seven shows over two weekends. How was I going to feel about everything being over?
I arrived down in the music room for our pre-show meeting and all of my pit orchestra kids were there with a dozen roses and a restaurant gift certificate...for me! It was unbelievable! I almost cried—I never expected anything so special! We said a prayer before we went up to the theatre, just like we had nine days ago when we opened the show. That was neat, too. At the end of the show, all of the directors, tech people, and I also got flowers from the cast. It felt a little sentimental going through the show for the last time, but it felt very good to be done, too.

What can I say about the musical? It was probably both the best and worst experience of my first year of teaching. It was the worst when I had my credibility challenged, when I was overwhelmed and consumed, or when I felt the show would never come together. It was the best when I sensed a connection with my students. At the highest points, I thought I was really making a difference and felt I was actually teaching the students something lifelong and valuable. It took quite a bit of reflection on my part to finally realize that some of the best and worst moments of the musical experience were in fact the exact same moments....Think about your own negative experiences as a teacher and I am confident you will probably come to that same conclusion: sometimes the worst situations, in retrospect, are actually positive, educational growth experiences in disguise.

Spring break was scheduled conveniently after the monumental task of the musical was complete, which was fine with everyone I came in contact with. I enjoyed some time away and returned with a renewed energy with which to face upcoming challenges.

March 12

Back to school after spring break—a little difficult, to say the least. There is a choir concert in nine days, so we'll all have to get in gear for that. Solo and ensemble contest for vocalists, strings, and piano is this Saturday, so there will be big performances for the String Ensemble and Show Choir at that event. Last week right before break I had to have another teacher sub for my Fundamentals class, and found out today that the teacher didn't have the students do the assignment I asked. In fact, it sounds like they didn't do much of anything, so now I'm behind where I wanted to be with them. It's not a big deal, I guess it's just the principle of it.

March 13 - Tuesday

Today the uniform rep measured all the band kids for our new uniforms! Dr. V. signed the order, so it's very much official! It is definitely a big accomplishment for my first year of teaching, but it never would have happened without the help of the band parents. We are also starting a flower bulb fundraiser, writing letters to possible donors, etc., to help start paying for the project. Needless to say, trying to run a rehearsal with all of these things going on was challenging and the kids were very inattentive. Plus I developed a big headache that started first thing in the morning once the uniform guy arrived. I was very stressed about all the decisions that had to be made: what additions I want

on the drum major's uniform, what I think
our street marching banner should look like,
etc. The school will have to live with whatever
I decide on for a long time, so I want everything
to be perfect.

I am also concerned with the Show Choir.
They perform at Solo and Ensemble on Saturday
and I'm not sure how they're going to do.
Actually, the whole choral side of the music
department has such a lack of focus since
the musical. It's like a lot of them feel they
don't have to do anything for the rest of
the school year since they participated in
the musical...really irritating.

I learned a lot about how to conduct an effective
rehearsal amongst distractions on this particular day.
I don't think I did a really great job of these things
at the time, but I know now what to do in the future
to make it better. First of all, don't hesitate to ask for
help from parents. In my situation, the students were
measured for their uniforms during band class time.
While you are busy with the business of educating
their children, available parents can help the uni-
form/fundraising representative measure students,
hand out supplies, or whatever needs to be done.
You should not divide your attention by trying to
run two or more activities at once, because nothing
will receive its due focus. Secondly, try not to make
a major production out of these extra-curricular
activities going on during rehearsal time. Of course

it is exciting to order new uniforms or concert attire, or to begin a new project, such as fund-raising. However, your main job as a music educator is to *teach* music. (As obvious as that sounds, I think many of us forget that from time to time). Encourage your students to be as attentive as possible. Make the process of what is happening this particular day clearly understood. For example, if you want the students to leave the room by section, two at a time, to be measured for their uniforms and rejoin rehearsal quietly when they are finished, then say that. Make your expectations known in a confident and organized manner, and the students should follow your lead.

My concern with the choirs is probably a universal problem. How do you keep students motivated after they have successfully completed a huge task such as the musical? I don't think I have a good answer to this situation, but I do have the experience to at least let you know what I faced and the things I tried. It is important to note here that not all of my vocal students acted in the immature manner I discussed in my journal entry; however, it was a significant enough number to change the dynamics of the ensembles. I especially had problems keeping the show choir on task: a good number of Seniors were enrolled in this ensemble, who traditionally seem to begin checking out at this point of the school year. The show choir also did that musical revue production back in December, so they seemed to think they had paid their dues to the music department for the year. I tried vigorously to let them know that was not the case.

When I spoke with the choirs about this issue, my plan was to appeal to them on many fronts. In preparing for solo and ensemble contest, I tried to sell them on what a different experience it was compared to anything else they had done. As we started new pieces for spring and continued things we had been working on for our upcoming March concert, I stressed that we still had music to make—the year was far from over. I reminded them that only a certain percentage of choral students had been in the musical; these upcoming performances were as important to other students, to the school, and to the music department as the musical was. Lastly, of course I reminded them that their grade was at stake if they decided not to participate fully and follow the expectations of the class.

At the least, the situation was disheartening. It made me both angry and sad to witness bright, talented students succumb to laziness and mediocrity. Some of them snapped out of it; others floated between giving a forced effort and simply taking up space. It hurt to see students care about nothing except themselves simply because they were worn out and unwilling to give anymore. You as a teacher no doubt give of yourself every day, and continue to do so even when you are tired, depressed, or angry. To not receive this effort in return, to me, is agonizing.

I don't know if this last idea is a possibility, but I've always thought that maybe the schedule of these big productions could determine ups and downs of students' attitude problems and help avoid negativity altogether. For example, what would've happened if the show choir's musical revue was scheduled at the end of the year, perhaps in May? Would they have fallen flat on their faces, or would they have been motivated after the big February musical by a new challenge? The truth is, I'm not sure. Every group of students, every year, in every situation is a little bit different and they respond accordingly. What works wonderfully one year may be disastrous the next. My advice is to simply experiment and see what situations become the most successful for you and your students.

March 14

Today was an in-service day—always nice to have time to see the other teachers. The shortened classes, while you don't have time to accomplish a lot, makes the day go fast; it's a nice change from routine. However, since Jazz Band is over one of the lunch hours it was its normal length. We got our judge's comment cards back from Solo and Ensemble contest so we read and discussed those and had a good rehearsal on some of our newer pieces. Planned and played a music history version of "Family Feud" in Fundamentals as a review for their quiz on Friday and it actually turned out really well.

> Tonight my fiancé and I went to this new community band rehearsal for the first time. He is a musician too, a trumpet player, so I think it will be something fun for us to do together. I had a good time playing in a band again—I forgot what it's like since now I'm on the other side of the podium all the time! My chops were even a bit sore, but I do miss playing!

I think it is very important to keep performing in addition to teaching. As I became a more permanent member of this community band, I realized how much it was helping me musically. I learned many things by watching other conductors. I was able to listen more for tuning and blend from within an ensemble instead of only in front of it. By playing things on my own instrument, my sight-reading and rhythm recognition was only getting faster and more accurate. Obviously, I had a great deal of experience with such things during college, but as real life teaching responsibilities took over, sometimes these things fall behind grading assignments, paperwork and meetings. We are so busy making sure that our *students* can perform, we forget about our *own* musical growth and enrichment. Now I have made my own personal musicianship more of a priority. On occasion, when my lesson plans are done, I try to use available prep time to practice. I make more time for musical things that are important to me. Try performing at your church, or join a community band or choir. It will take a time commitment, but it's worth it. I firmly believe that if you don't do this, you may forget why you are in the business of music education to begin with.

March 15

Back to the sectional lesson schedule today—I gave the band a break after Large Group and through spring break. Makes for a long day for me, but it was nice to get the students back in that sectional environment. Had final rehearsals for the String Ensemble and Show Choir before contest on Saturday. I think they will both do well—they were really focused today. Chorus wasn't bad either—I added a student from String Ensemble to play the violin part for our "Schindler's List" piece. For the first time everything was put together, it went okay— there were some tempo problems and the usual piano player problems, but hopefully it will all come together for the concert. It's not like I can make them practice.

Probably the neatest part of my day was the two meetings I had: one with the Advancement office people and other with the teachers who are going on the Senior class retreat. With Advancement, I am trying to get different ideas for musical partnerships going with the area grade school students and teachers to increase enrollment and help recruit students to our high school. It

---

will be a long but exciting process! I am also looking forward to being a part of the three-day retreat for the Senior class. It will be like a camp where I am a counselor, which I have done before. I miss doing that, so I hope it will be a good experience.

March 16 – Friday

I can't believe how much energy I've had this week! The first week back to school after spring break and without "Fiddler" has been pretty nice for the energy level. I'm not burned out, I'm glad it's Friday, and I'll actually have some ambition to do something social this weekend!

I made it an easier day for myself with individual practicing and sectionals in Chamber Ensemble and Jazz Band, yet I feel those activities were productive, too. Concert Choir mostly paid attention today since their concert is next week. As usual, I think it's amazing that they think they will pull off a decent concert by only paying attention the last three rehearsals before a concert.

I gave a test to my Fundamentals class today on the Baroque era in music history. Most of them blew through it and turned it in so fast that I knew they were going to get a bunch of things wrong...and they did. It was like most of them didn't even listen the last few weeks at all. I didn't want it to

> be a hard test and I didn't purposely put things on the test to trick them, but I did expect them to know basic concepts. It was so frustrating and disappointing. I decided to "curve" the test—instead of grading it out of 100 points I will grade it out of 90 points since the highest grade was an 89. That seems more than fair....

The worst part about the failure of most students on that test was the fact that I had to admit to myself that it was my failure, too. Of course, there is responsibility placed on the individual student to study, to listen in class, to take notes, to do assignments, etc. But I feel a good teacher also takes responsibility for the knowledge they pass on (or do not) to their students. I don't believe in saying, "Well, they didn't learn it. Too bad, that's not my fault."

Granted, I felt I did a lot of things to set them up to succeed. I attempted to make class interactive and did not merely lecture to the students. I always reviewed ideas we discussed in the previous class and I tried to help them make connections. We played that game I talked about in my journal to aid them in their review for the test. Yet it still didn't seem to be enough to reach them at the level I desired. I mentioned before that a good number of students in this music fundamentals class were below average students to begin with. Some never even took notes throughout the entire year. I believe several students out of the eleven simply enrolled in the class because they thought it would be a cakewalk. So, I guess I can't say I was surprised by some of the low test scores, but still I was frustrated.

If you find yourself in this situation, try some of the things I did. Never be afraid to call parents. Tell them exactly what is or is not happening with their child in your class. If you call home and tell parents that their son or daughter did poorly on an exam, they will probably be concerned. You should be able to back that information up with other facts about their behavior in class, lack of note-taking skills or other factors which, in your professional opinion, may have contributed to their stumbling grade. I also advocate the use of student-to-teacher conferences. After a test, whether a student earns an "A" or an "F," schedule a time to spend five minutes talking with each student about it. Ask questions, such as, "How are you doing?" "Is there anything I can help you with?" or "What happened on this test?" This could bring you to a more personal and understanding level with the student and perhaps guide them in other aspects of his or her life besides music history. Lastly, never stop trying new things. If certain techniques didn't work to successfully teach them the last unit, find new and exciting ways to introduce and teach new material. Games, puzzles and other strange assignments sometimes work in mysterious ways.

As for me, I implemented some of these ideas

with moderate success. A few kids simply didn't seem to care no matter what I tried, but I managed to help others improve their grade on future music history tests and projects. I tried my best and reached those I could. While it may not seem like it, especially to those of us who are perfectionists, this is indeed a victory.

March 17 - Saturday - Solo and Ensemble

It was mostly a very good day. Lots of kids were scheduled at the same time—there were no conflicts for them, but it made it impossible for me to see many of their solos. I saw as many as I could and parents commented on the importance of my support, so it was nice to feel appreciated.

The String Ensemble did great. I could tell many of the students were nervous as we waited outside our performance site. When it was time, we took our place in the room, tuned, and off we went. They played the piece the best I ever heard it! Our judge was very pleasant and complimentary, and there were lots of happy spectators in the room with us who applauded and whistled after our performance. What a neat experience! We got a first!

The one downer of the day was the Show Choir earning a second. They were rated excellent in almost every musical category, but we didn't do choreography, so that knocked us

down. I don't know how the group is going to
feel when we talk about it back at school, but
I feel terrible, like I'm personally responsible.
The contest handbook of rules doesn't say
anything about choreography being one of
the things they are judged on, but does the
term "show choir" make it a given? How am I
supposed to know, especially as a first-year
teacher whose area of expertise has never
been show choirs? Should I have called and
asked? I feel bad, but I'm trying not to let
it overshadow the good things I've done
today, like the String performance.

So, I guess I screwed up. The show choir kids
were understanding when I explained what happened.
They agreed…how should any of us know what the
rules are unless they were printed in the festival
handbook? The truth is, they don't like dancing that
much anyway and were actually quite happy and sat-
isfied with their vocal performance at the contest. I
still felt like it was something I should have known
in order to help them succeed fully…when in doubt,
find out.

March 19

Monday—fun to congratulate all the Solo
and Ensemble kids, write up the announcement

to tell ratings over the intercom, and satisfying to get all the students' medals and
awards ordered today. It was not as fun to
get ready for the choral concert this Wednesday.
I am getting very little cooperation. I can't
believe it—the Chorus especially has had
their music since before Christmas and some
of them can hardly sing it. So frustrating.
Doesn't help that some of them don't give
any effort, that they think the musical theatre performances fulfilled their singing
obligations for the year. I'm trying my best,
but it's not good enough because I don't
know how to get through to them. Conversely,
the String Ensemble is very pleased with
themselves, as they should be, because of
their first rating in the festival on Saturday.
I am very proud of them, too. They have
really improved and grown over the past
seven months, which makes me feel good.

March 20

My life never gets boring—the kids make
sure of that. Last week, while I was at the
Senior Retreat meeting after school in the
conference room up by the main office, there
was a physical and verbal fight in the music
room between two junior boys. I finally
found out about it from the assistant principal.
One is a guitar player in Jazz Band and one
is a bass player who isn't. It's been a fairly
big deal the last week or so because the

> fight has continued and escalated into
> threatening e-mails between the two. Plus it
> brings up supervision issues in the room
> itself. I've always left the music room unlocked
> after school, even if I have to run somewhere
> quickly. This allows kids to pick up their
> instruments, socialize, or whatever; then I
> always lock it when I leave for the day.
> Can't I do that anymore because of a few
> disruptive students? It's like I can't trust
> them unsupervised for a moment. In the
> past, everyone has been okay, no equipment
> was broken, but now with this new issue I'll
> have to be a lot more vigilant.

As we discussed before, the music department is like no other place in the school. Some students base their entire social and academic existence out of the band, choral, or orchestra rehearsal room. There are many reasons for this: they love their friends, they love you, they love music, and/or they generally feel comfortable surrounded by pianos and music stands. However, when an issue like the above takes place, all the rules change. When the primary safety of students is threatened, all of a sudden convenience and social fun doesn't seem that crucial.

The first action I took when I was in this situation was to ban the non-music student involved in the fight from my classroom. Normally, I would never think about denying a student the opportunity to access the school's music department, but this situation made it a necessity. Apparently, these two students had "personality conflicts" in the past as well, and since I cannot very well ban my jazz band guitar player from the room, a good solution seemed to give then a place where they cannot run into each other.

Secondly, I increased my own level of awareness as to what was going on in the music department, especially at times when before I really hadn't paid close attention, such as before and after school. The way I saw it, those were my times to get work done, to wind down from the day or to gear up for it, and the students' time to be relaxed and social without me staring them in the face. Sometimes the last thing I needed to hear was more teenage chatter. But after the fight occurred, I monitored the entire social scene in the music room much more carefully. Obviously, the fight would not have happened if I was there, or if it would have started, I could have possibly "channeled" their energies more effectively. Now, I listen to and participate in student conversations a bit more, peek my head out of my office to say "good morning," and generally remind those who need it of my presence. So far, no other confrontations have occurred, so I hope it was a one-time incident and that my heightened awareness makes a difference.

March 21

Day of reckoning for the choirs with their spring concert tonight. I felt like the Chorus was really trying hard today, but they still had a bad rehearsal. Maybe they will realize they need to start trying before the day of the concert next time. The Show Choir was pretty organized and ready for tonight.

The Concert Band was just a bunch of brats today—don't know what their problem was. I am really nervous about which songs they're going to be able to play at their spring concert in two weeks. Obviously our three from Large Group are fine, but that festival was over a month ago. Even with spring break in there, we should be able to prepare something new. We can't stagnate for a month! They just haven't been focusing at all. Plus, the Band has this flower bulb fundraiser going on to raise money for the new uniforms and I don't think enough students are taking it seriously. How can I motivate them?

One would think that the idea of new uniforms and looking great would be motivation enough. However, when any school group has fundraisers, often there are "incentives" for selling the highest amount of a product, such as cash, movie passes, or little stuffed animals. Personally, I do not believe in this practice for high school students for a number of reasons. First of all, I don't believe most high school students are even motivated by winning plastic toys. Secondly, the cost of incentives for fundraising takes away from your profit. But perhaps most important is the fact that I believe young adults should possess, or be taught to possess, the intrinsic motivation to contribute their efforts to a cause which ultimately benefits them. Are we teaching kids today anything if we are not teaching them to be contributing members of society?

Perhaps I am overreacting here, but please allow me to remain on my soapbox for another paragraph or two and indulge these ideas for a moment. Are kids today spoiled? Every week, it seems a new study flashes across the television or newspaper about how children today have more "stuff" than some of us had even as adults years ago. How do many of them obtain these material things? Their parents give it to them...or give them an obscene one hundred dollar per week allowance. Maybe this teaches them to manage money, but I have a hunch about what else it teaches them. In my view, it screams at them that they don't have to work to earn anything; that everything will come easy for them. While the situation is very different at an inner city or extremely rural area, think about the scenario at the school I teach at: as a private, suburban school, parents pay tuition of over five thousand dollars per year. While a good number of students receive some financial assistance, it remains an upper class school. Designer clothes are the norm. Many students drive cars newer than mine to school— I even see a Corvette or two in the student lot. You cannot convince me that students are earning the money to pay for this with their ten hour per week job at the mall.

You may already see how this connects to my fundraiser project with the marching band uniforms. If students' parents act as though money is no object, why should the child bust their butt going door to door selling flower bulbs or candy bars? If a solid work ethic has never been instilled at home, what chance do I have as a teacher, coming into a student's life at their fifteenth birthday, and convincing them to work hard and raise money? If kids see how things are merely given to them their whole life, why should these new uniforms be any different?

The truth is, I didn't do a very good job of motivating the band kids to sell for the fundraiser and I don't think incentives would have helped much. I hate feeling defeated or giving up, but all of the above factors seemed to work against me. I had a couple of conversations with the group as a whole, but what I thought were inspirational words seemed to fall on deaf ears. Of course not all of my students fell into this category; in fact, some were great flower bulb salespeople. At the end of the sale, we raised a good amount of money: almost one thousand dollars. But it could have been so much more profitable with better attitudes and participation. In short, I bring this situation to your attention so that you might be aware of the social and economic state at your own school and prepared for how it may affect your department.

The choral concert went pretty well, considering how much I was dreading it. Most students controlled their apathy for the night and put on a good show. The Chorus pulled together nicely on the "Schindler's List" piece with piano and violin accompaniment, and there were great moments with the other ensembles as well. The concert was short and sweet, about 45 minutes, which was fine since most parents had sat through a three-hour musical less than a month ago. I also took the opportunity to announce the Solo and Ensemble and Large Group choral ratings, so the audience liked that.

March 22

Thursday—last day of the week and of the quarter—I can't believe it's the end of the third quarter! I worked feverishly the last few days to get my grades done so I don't have to use the teacher work day tomorrow...I can have a 3-day weekend just like the students! Spent some time in Concert Choir today discussing the concert and got some good responses, but others didn't really care. I stress time and time again the importance of evaluation—not just doing something and moving on, but thinking about what they are doing well and what we can improve on. I hope some of them see the value of doing that in other aspects of their lives as well.

March 26

This week will be an even shorter week of classes for me than last week. I will only be in school today and Tuesday, then the rest of the week I will be at a retreat center out in the woods with other teachers and the Senior class for their 3-day retreat. However, next week is the spring instrumental concert, so I feel like I really have to make strong impressions and lead solid rehearsals to last until we meet again next week. At the moment, I'm still disturbed with the Concert Band. We did so well on the pieces we did for Large Group, but we had a long time to work on them—from after Christmas until the end of February. I've wanted to add a piece or two to our program this last month, but it's been difficult. I also don't like the pressure of having to put something together in such a short amount of time...at least, it seems like a short time with spring break and musical theatre obligations stuck in there. Whatever we do for the upcoming concert, I don't want it to sound like it was thrown together.

The Show Choir really pissed me off today also. Here I come into class and give them exactly what they wanted: the choice of which pieces in the school music library they were going to work on for the rest of the year. All I wanted from them was to pay attention. Instead, a lot of them talked practically the whole class period, didn't follow

> along with the music, and didn't seem to be
> listening. I finally asked them, and quite harshly,
> "Why should I give you this privilege if you
> can't even listen?" Then, like ironic clockwork,
> the bell rang. So I told them as they were
> packing up that we would have a further discussion
> about it next week. I don't understand—wouldn't
> they be more tuned in and attentive when
> given choices about music? It really made
> me crabby.

Sometimes I just can't figure kids out. In the above situations with both the band and the show choir, I tried to make them the best they could be and it seemed as though most of them fought me every step of the way. If you find yourself in this situation as well, try something that was only recently recommended to me by a fellow teacher: be honest with your students and tell them how you feel. It is so simple, but I never really gave it a lot of thought before. Level with your students and let them know how their actions make you feel or how they affect the class' atmosphere or productivity. For example, I should have told the band some of the same things I wrote in my journal, such as, "You know, I've been trying really hard to get us ready for this concert. I really think we need to add another piece to our program. If we don't, it's like we are stagnating and haven't learned anything new since the end of February. I don't think any of us want that. So, let's all work together and buckle down to make this spring concert the best we can." It might have worked to tell the show choir, "Look ladies and gentlemen, this is what you are saying to me by your actions. Perhaps you don't mean to, but this is how I feel you are affecting our goals...." I tried some of this communication style since these occasions and most times it has the desired result: students examine their behavior from an outside perspective and usually see things a bit more logically and responsibly. It was scary for me at first to share my expectations and feelings of hurt and disappointment with a room full of teenagers; as in any situation like this, we open ourselves up to ridicule and rejection. But in my experience, kids are accepting and appreciative to this kind of honesty and concern.

March 27

Day before retreat, my last day of con-ventional teaching for the week. It was kinda tough for me to focus, not to mention adding to everything here at school that my fiancé and I are closing on our new house this weekend!

Tried to stress today, like I did with the groups who met yesterday, how close the instrumental spring concert really is. I'm nervous about going on retreat and not being with my ensembles for the rest of the week. Hopefully, they will practice and use their

time wisely with the help of whoever subs
for my classes. Busy with other things besides
those lesson plans, also. I guess my grades
didn't export correctly into the computer
system, so I had to work with the office to
fix that. I also wrote letters to all my Seniors
for them to receive during the retreat. It
was something that all teachers were encour-
aged to do and I thought it was a great idea,
to write each Senior we knew a letter of
encouragement and good luck. It took a lot
of time the last few days, but I hope it will
be worth it and that it will mean something
to them.

March 28-30 – Senior Retreat

Well, what can I say about Senior
Retreat...most of it was a great experience;
I'm really glad I could be a part of it. Each
teacher who went was a small group leader.
The groups each had about ten kids. We led
discussions and activities with on several
different occasions over the three days. My
small group was wonderful; we had some
really touching talks. Most kids got really
deep and emotional—some girls even cried!
The large group sessions I witnessed were
powerful, too. They really seemed to strike
a nerve with the kids because we addressed
topics like social goodness, popularity, hurts,
forgiveness, etc. My hope is that the kids
really take these concerns to heart.

The retreat was fun for me because I got the opportunity to become closer to a lot of other teachers. This was important to me because I don't see many other teachers that often: whereas every other teacher in the school is part of a "department" and collaborates or merely sees their colleagues on an every day basis, I don't have that professional and social luxury.

If the retreat was simply fun and games, then I wouldn't have a lot to write about. But if you know kids, you know there has to be some stories. We as teachers caught kids smoking almost constantly: in their rooms, in the woods, and practically out in the open. I've never seen so many "children" smoking in my entire life...and they think they look so cool. It was just sickening. But apparently since most of them are eighteen years old, it is legal and we can't do much about it.

The most "exciting" thing I was a part of during retreat was catching a strip poker game. Another teacher and I were doing random room checks the second night of the retreat and found about sixteen kids in a room with about half of them actually playing—a few of them down to their bras or boxers. The other teacher started yelling at them, demanding to know what was going on. Most of them stared like deer in headlights; others started trying to cover up. She yelled at me to run and get the school ministry leader who was in charge of the retreat while she stood in the doorway, making sure nobody ran off.

From that point on, the night was a complete disaster. All the other students were confined to their own rooms and the rest of the activities for the night were canceled. We made all the kids who were in the room call their parents and tell them what they were a part of. The whole process stunk—by the time they all called home, it was after 2 a.m. Then we sat up with them further and tried to talk through the situation with the group, deciding what their punishment would be. The worst part was that most of them seemed to feel no remorse. In fact, many were trying to justify their stupidity of playing strip poker on a religious school retreat. This made it even more frustrating for me to be up in the middle of night with them: a bunch of kids who seemed to have passed on the whole point of the retreat anyway. So, fine. At that point, the best punishment the team of teachers could come up with was to ban them from retreat activities for the rest of the trip. The next morning until the busses left, the perpetrators went to a supervised room away from their other classmates and sat in silence, missing out on the powerful conclusions to the retreat.

Some cried, some laughed it off. But administration sure did not laugh. The retreat coordinator called school the next morning and the principal imposed a 3-day suspension on all of the kids involved and is making them write apology letters to several parties involved, even me. At the least, the whole

I left the Senior retreat with lots of mixed emotions. It made me appreciate the wonder and potential of youth and doubt their future and character at the same time. In the scheduled group settings, both large and small, the progress of the students and their connections to life and the world were striking. Then during free times, we couldn't trust them. In a way, I feel as though we wasted our efforts. But then as I reflected further, I know we did not. We planted a seed that simply needs some time to fully take root and blossom. We helped give the Seniors a healthy mental and spiritual base to continue their journey into the adult world. Realistically, the seed will probably not flourish in every student, but at least each was given the chance and opportunity.

Logistically, even though I am not in charge of planning the retreat, there are some things I would request to be done differently if I were going to counsel at it again. Maybe these ideas will help you if you have a similar experience on the horizon for your students. For example, the smoking thing really bothered me. I think the whole experience should be non-smoking for everyone, regardless of age, just like a regular school campus is. Of course, you don't want kids sneaking off into the woods to smoke and starting a forest fire, but rules are rules. Make it clear that they will not bring cigarettes or any drugs or alcohol on the trip—if they are even found with it, they will be sent home. Maybe that would encourage kids to be sneaky, but backing up the rule with diligent supervision could work wonders.

Secondly, during our Senior retreat, males and females were allowed in each other's rooms until a certain hour of the night. At the two other camps where I've been a counselor, males and females were *never* allowed in each other's rooms and that is the policy I would recommend at our school's next Senior retreat. You would like to trust them and treat them as adults, but the sad fact is that some kids cannot handle that trust. The retreat facility we used had two gymnasiums, the dining hall where we all ate, lounges and several game rooms. The way I see it, that leaves plenty of places for guys and gals to see each other and spend time together that are public and relatively free of trouble or temptation.

If you are planning an event like this for your school, hang tough. I don't mean to make you apprehensive, but so many negative things can happen if everything is not planned out and discussed extensively ahead of time. Implement clear rules as well as consequences if those rules are broken. Inform students, parents, other teachers, and administration of these policies and ask for their help and support in the enforcement of those rules. Try to conjure up any circumstance and have an answer as to how you would handle it. It is a big responsibility to lead a class trip or retreat, but there can be some great rewards as well. Good luck!

And best wishes to all as we continue our journey into April....

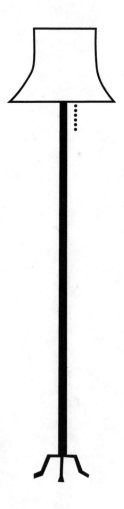

April

For me, April was when the days really started to uncontrollably fly by. It seems as though there is so little time until the end of the school year, yet there are still so many things to do, such as spring concerts, planning for graduation, and other year-end events. I found myself starting to tie up loose ends from earlier in the school year, such as making sure pep band music and shirts were turned in, as well as looking through the music library to get a head start on ideas for next school year. By this time, you may find yourself thinking you're an old pro at this music education business. But believe me, there are still many surprises, adventures, and learning experiences out there for you to discover.

April 2

Back to school after the Senior Retreat and a full weekend of moving into the new house! It is such an amazing feeling to be a homeowner—I love the house! It's hard to be here at school since there are so many things to be done at the house...my thoughts keep drifting back there. It's nice to be able to walk to school and to get fresh air in the morning, plus the days seem shorter since it's quicker to get home.
Most classes seemed to go well last week

with their respective substitutes—I was especially worried about the instrumental classes because of our concert this week. The String Ensemble really had the Monday morning blues. It took us five times to start our piece from Solo and Ensemble correctly! Considering we earned a first on it a few weeks ago, that was disheartening. Focus! How do you achieve that right away on a Monday morning? Show Choir, taking into account their little attitude problem last week, was well-behaved and attentive today after finalizing the music they chose for the rest of the year.

Since many of you reading this book are young adults and upcoming professionals, perhaps you are in the same situation I was: being in the market for purchasing your first home. While I am not an expert on the subject and it is a far cry from advice on music education, allow me to tell you a few things about my experience that may help you.

First of all, the process of shopping for and ultimately purchasing a house, condominium, or other property is an experience like no other. You will feel many different and contradicting emotions, from elated to depressed, from anxious to overwhelmed. Try to keep these feelings in check, keep things in perspective, and refuse to be talked into anything.

My biggest piece of advice for you is to strongly consider buying a home relatively close to your school.

While you may have heard all the horror stories about nosy parents keeping tabs on your private life and have therefore vowed to live in a completely different zip code than your school, consider these facts. Before I lived in the house two blocks from school, I had an apartment in a neighboring suburb. It took me thirty minutes to drive one way, and that was only if the traffic was good. When I had concerts, pep band engagements, or other after school/evening activities, I had to drive that time and distance twice a day...or not go home at all until very late at night. Maybe you like that much driving, but personally I would rather be at my home doing any number of activities which I enjoy much more, such as reading, cooking, playing with my dog, or simply relaxing and talking with my future spouse.

Seriously weigh all of the physical, financial, and emotional factors when considering making one of the biggest investments of your life. Good luck and enjoy the ride!

April 3

Pretty typical day, if there is such a thing. It was interesting to talk with the group of teachers whom I usually have lunch with, when I actually do get up to the lounge, about the scandal on Senior retreat. It was kinda fun to be the one who was "in the know" about things. Jazz Band had a good

---

rehearsal and sounds ready for the concert this Thursday. I received a bad report from the sub who had my Fundamentals class last week; apparently they wouldn't do their assignment and decided to talk and screw around the whole time instead. I really yelled at them...then I gave them a pop quiz, which most of them flunked, of course. I got the programs done for the concert, finally got caught up on phone calls and messages from being gone, so in general, I felt good about getting things accomplished today.

April 4 - Wednesday

The entire week is going fast! I'm not sure if that's because I have a lot going on between unpacking at home and the spring instrumental concert or what. The String Ensemble still has some problems, which was unnerving with the concert tomorrow night. Even some of the string students were getting on the cases of the ones who were screwing up! I think that was a good thing—it may be a little rude or intimidating, but it shows they care about the quality of the ensemble.

I don't know if I would encourage kids "ripping on" other kids about their musical performance in class, but it sure was a neat experience when it happened.

For once, I wasn't the only one who pointed out faults, envisioned better music, or spoke out against mediocrity. The kids, while maybe not the most tactful or polite, finally voiced the care and concern I invested all year. It felt good.

At the time, I really didn't know what to say about the comments. I simply looked at everyone, took a deep breath and said, "Okay, let's fix this," and continued the rehearsal. If given another chance, I would spend a couple of moments fixing the mental environment as well as the musical one. I may ask my star viola player to describe what he heard that he didn't like…and constructively this time. When he would then talk about the inaccurate second violins, I would ask them if that was indeed the problem and if there was something I could do to help them. By positively addressing the concerns yourself and encouraging others to do the same, you show students that there are more successful ways of dealing with problems than complaining or putting others down.

April 5

Day of concert, but I feel pretty good about it. Even though I had to yell at the Jazz Band to focus and quit talking so much, we had a good rehearsal and should sound great. Chamber Ensemble also had a successful final run before tonight.

Couple of other neat things happened

---

today. A Senior saxophone player who has been a great leader and fantastic musician all year asked for some music from me, so I gave him a movement of a piece I worked on for my college senior recital. He started playing it during one of his study halls today, and I was lucky enough to have a prep period at the same time. We talked about the piece a little and I listened to him later from my office. It was a cool feeling. Ever since the retreat, this student has been even more friendly and helpful—he even wrote me a response letter to the one I sent him on the retreat. It feels so great to bond with kids like that.

April 6

Friday and after a concert—did some productive but low-key things. Watched the concert video, wrote evaluations. In general, the concert went well and I received several great comments from parents. The Jazz Band put on a good show and has really improved since the beginning of the year. Not only have they grown, but we've also had a lot more time to practice the pieces than at the beginning of the year. Concert Band and Strings also did well—things like crescendos and accents that they never seem to do in rehearsal all of a sudden magically appear in concert. Details always make the difference.

> Chamber music has played better, but they
> sounded okay.
>   All in all, it's been rewarding to be part
> of the process of the kids growing together
> throughout the year. Is that what has to
> happen every year? And if that's the case, how
> do you build the program to make it better?
> How do you make the music program grow
> more quickly? Or does it just take time and
> happen eventually with a helping teacher
> who is a continuous element in the school?
> The compliments after the concert were
> really great and make (almost) everything
> negative that happens worthwhile. But my
> "rush" of performing is not as strong as it
> once was and I don't get that nervous any-
> more. Is that a bad sign, or is it a sign of
> my growth and position of leadership? I
> don't know....

Of course, I should have been happy with my successes for the year to date, but always the perfectionist, I was looking for more. I achieved "A," now I was sick of it and wanted "B." Which is not necessarily a bad thing; however, don't let your quest for what is over the horizon overshadow the good things that are right at your feet.

The growth of a music program is an issue at most schools, especially private or rural area schools. While I could speak about recruitment ideas or enrollment boosting strategies, those factors are still rather uncontrollable. They deal with other people and outside sources. You may realize by now that the only thing you really can control is yourself and your own actions and behaviors (and that's even a stretch sometimes). I feel that one of the most successful ways to build a music program rests with you as the teacher and the things you plan and accomplish with your students. Who knows how great you, your program, or your kids are if you are never showcased? For example, as my first year of teaching progressed, I found more and more people saying things to me like, "Marching in that parade was cool, we never did anything like that last year," or, "I think going to that singing competition was a good experience for the kids." I made the various experiences a priority, planned them, and prepared the students to do the best we knew how.

While your students may not be wonderful performers at first, it is essential to get them out in the community and be seen. School concerts are great, but usually parents account for the highest percentage of the crowd. Try to get your concert publicized in the local paper. Go to competitions, parades, and festivals. Put the news about what you did at these events in the school bulletin. You will be surprised at how the word of what you are doing will spread like wildfire. Quality obviously counts, but effort goes a long way as well. And it all starts with you and your own effort, enthusiasm, and dedication.

April 9

I watched "Oprah" today when I got home
from school and the topic of the show was
finding your passion and carrying through
with working on it. Is teaching and making
music my passion? Yes, I think so—it makes
me feel good, I'm good at it, and I try my
best to bring that passion to my students.
But sometimes, it is difficult to carry through
with that when you have the battles of attitudes, paperwork, and other aspects of everyday
life. I am also passionate about writing and
really want to turn these random journal
entries into a useful book. The show said
that all it takes is making the first moves.
Today I continued showing the video of
the concert to the instrumental groups who
hadn't seen it yet. I think it provided some
good insights. Made headway in other classes
as well: the new music in Concert Choir is
starting to come together. Students were
listening pretty attentively to the "stories"
I was telling about Haydn and Mozart in
Fundamentals of Music.

One of the greatest educational tools I discovered is the value of telling stories. Everyone loves a
story, fiction or non-fiction, about another place or
time. Stories can be interesting and fun or sad and
heartfelt. However, in order to be most useful, they
must relate back to the topic you are teaching. I

highly suggest you begin a collection of worthwhile stories to share with your students. For example, talk about a composer's personal life or research the debut of pieces your ensembles are playing. The background knowledge and imagery a story provides make concepts more realistic to students. And if you look closely enough, there is a lesson to be learned in every tale.

April 10 – Tuesday

Why is it that whenever I have to do something "businesslike" in Concert Band, the kids go nuts? Today we spent about half the period turning in music and pep band shirts, which was fine—it had to be done. But afterwards, when it was time for rehearsal, the kids wouldn't settle down. They had time to relax and talk with their friends for the first part of the hour, then they couldn't get to work. How do I get them to be able to switch gears more effectively?

Even though I didn't know how long it was going to take to finish the "housecleaning" matters, I probably still should have scheduled class the other way around: rehearsal first, business later.

On the flip side, I am always impressed with the String Ensemble. I gave them some sectional time at the beginning of class to

---

refresh their memories on a couple pieces
we had not looked at in a while, and they
were very efficient and hardworking. What
is the difference between Band and Strings
anyway? Is Band rowdier because there are
more students? Is Strings more refined
because that is the stereotypical image of
orchestral players? I'm sure there isn't only
one reason.

April 11

   Today was this month's in-service day,
which I always like. I enjoy talking to the
rest of the faculty in the morning during
meetings, and the twenty-minute class schedule is kinda nice. It's fast paced, yet I still
usually get a lot accomplished with my students.
At the meeting, we had a good speaker who
talked about how girls change as they grow
into adolescence, then those of us from the
Senior retreat had a meeting to debrief
about the whole experience. I thought it
was worthwhile to get together with all the
faculty from retreat again and talk about
what we can do differently to make next
year's retreat better—I was more than
happy to put my "two cents" in....
   Jazz Band had a great rehearsal—we are
really digging into a new and difficult piece
called "Beyond the Sea" that switches between
a swing and Latin feel. Other classes were

> good, too—today was the last time I'll see
> my "B day" classes until after Easter break,
> so I tried to do a good job of reviewing things.
> Hopefully, I sent them into the vacation
> with a good understanding of the music.

On Thursday, the last day before Easter vacation, there was a school assembly. The main purpose of it was to send off the Academic Decathlon team to the state competition. However, I also requested a spot in the assembly so I could introduce the musicians who qualified for the state Solo and Ensemble festival because of their superior performances at the district festivals in March. It was fun for me to speak in front of the student body and salute my highest achieving musicians. I felt it was important for them to get the recognition they deserved for their hard work. Sometimes, it is difficult to watch athletes or Academic Decathlon students receive the constant praise they do. A good number of my musicians strive just as hard, if not more so, yet are oftentimes not validated. I encourage you as their teacher to be an advocate, a voice to shout for their publicity and acclaim.

> April 23
>
> Having a week off after Easter Sunday
> was a nice break. It was a chance to

recharge and get ready for the big push to the end of the school year. However, now that I'm back, I realize what a short time we have to prepare for things that are coming up. The combined spring concert is less than three weeks away, yet still a lot of music seems practically new to the ensembles. The break was wonderful, but it's like it put the whole music department a couple of steps back as far as preparing for upcoming events. I think we will rebound, but we have to get back into the groove quickly. How do you engage kids in school after they've spent a week in the Bahamas? I had some kids skipping class today too, so the end of the year weirdness is definitely starting to kick in. Seniors were restless—hard to keep everyone focused.

No doubt, the day after a vacation, you are probably as lethargic as the students. The best piece of advice I have for you when coming back to school on a day after a vacation is to try not to show that. Replace it instead with creative energy and out-of-the-ordinary classroom activities. This would not be the day to do a "boring" lecture or a "ho-hum" rehearsal. This is the day to shake things up, take kids by surprise, and get them excited and energized. Try setting up the rehearsal room differently, make students move around and dance, or get out the hand-held percussion instruments and learn a new rhythm. Better yet, think up your own activities and tailor them especially for your students' needs and abilities.

April 24

Right away this morning, the day started on the wrong foot. Someone hung up a disgusting "joke," an illustrated picture and caption about another student, on the music department door. I really don't have time or energy for that stupidity, especially with the fight that occurred a while back, so I really yelled at everyone who happened to be hanging out in there at the time. They all looked pretty guilty. I think it's amazing what teenagers think is funny. So that put me in a funk right away. Plus, besides the spring concert, I'm realizing everything else that is happening in the next month: music department banquet, a fine arts night, the grade school solo and ensemble contest we are hosting, graduation. Nothing super-stressful by itself, but put all together...that's a different story.

I can't be that depressed though, because a lot of good things happened today as well. The Chorus did a good job rehearsing and we made some progress on all of our current songs. Also, very much to my surprise, the new band uniforms arrived today! Eleven huge cardboard boxes—it was exciting! Now the challenge will be organizing them all and putting them away. But it's a nice problem to have after all the hard work of getting them in the first place!

April 25

I left school yesterday with a headache and it hasn't gone away yet. Even though I've been having pretty good rehearsals and classes lately, that feels secondary. It's like I have two full-time jobs: teaching, then all this administrative stuff. And I'm almost more stressed and nervous now than I was at the beginning of the year. I want to keep every-body happy and send everyone away for the summer on a "good note." Even though I don't really feel like a new teacher anymore, I really still am because I haven't been through any of this stuff at the end of the year. Finally, I scheduled some time with Dr. V. today and actually talked about what was coming up and what my responsibilities were for the next month or so. That helped—I got the support I needed and I didn't have to wonder anymore. She gave me some encouragement and told me how great I was doing, so that felt good, too.

I know I've said it before, but it's so important that it's necessary to repeat: don't be afraid to ask questions! It's okay not to know everything! Don't make the mistake I made of stressing yourself out for days and making yourself sick over things that you're not sure about. I had no idea what was going to be expected of me for events such as graduation or fine arts night. My principal was a guiding force and either told me what I needed to know or pointed me in the right direction to seek the counsel of others. I think that many new professionals right out of college, teachers included, feel weak or stupid if they have to ask a question. I know because that was me at one time. Let go of these insecurities. It is only by asking these questions that we can become not only better in our profession, but also better people.

April 26 – Thursday

As the weather gets nicer and the weekdays get closer to the weekend, it's tougher and tougher to keep students focused. This is especially ill timed, considering the upcoming activities the music department has. I think the year has been successful, so I don't want anything bad to happen now. I know I must have been like this when I was in high school, too—I'm sure almost everyone is when spring comes...but how do I make the last six weeks of the school year engaging, not something to simply "get through?" Concert Band was very crazy today; I could hardly keep them focused on anything. The Strings were focused and quiet, they just can't play their music. We've had this certain piece since September and it still isn't coming together. Granted, it is difficult, but not beyond their abilities. I wonder how to get the kids to still want to achieve great things at this time of the school year.

April 27

Nice weather again plus it's the day before Prom, so lots of kids are skipping class and wandering all over school. I was even a victim myself during Fundamentals class. After the students were done with their tests, we were walking down the hall to use another classroom which had a television and VCR so we could continue watching the movie "Amadeus." Mr. G., the athletic director, came around a corner, saw the group of us and yelled, "Hey! Where are all you guys going?" Obviously, he thought we were skipping school and that I was a student! Hmph. Standing at the front of the group, I raised my hand slightly and said, "Umm, Mr. G., they're with me." He backed off in a huffy fashion as we walked into the empty classroom. I thought the confrontation was over, but he continued to stand in the doorway and look at us as I got the group set up to watch the movie. Then he said quite arrogantly, "K., why don't you wear some lipstick or something so I know that you're a teacher," and walked off.

I couldn't believe the sheer inappropriateness of the comment, especially in front of students. Some of my students looked at me inquisitively, but I purposely tried not to show a reaction on my face, even though it really pissed me off. What a jerk!

I hope you are never faced with a situation like the one above. I wouldn't go so far as to call it sexual harassment or anything, but it comes pretty darn close. Even though I'm sure the comment simply came as an attempt to cover up his own stupidity and shallowness, the remark, at least in my eyes, only made him look worse. As for me, it made me feel unimportant and unattractive, to say the least.

I didn't come forward to anyone at school about the comment until much later; in fact, it was the next school year. I ended up telling my story to the principal as a "character witness" for a coach who was also experiencing problems with the athletic director. While nothing significant came about after we told our stories, the situations were noted and documented. This becomes important if there are ever other incidents reported. I wish I would've told my story sooner. Not because I have a desire to see the athletic director fired, but by telling someone about it, I felt better. I also knew that I was making a difference and contributing to a more protected and healthy school environment. As a new teacher or a veteran teacher, no one should have to put up with that kind of degrading environment.

The next day, Saturday, was Prom. While I am not a huge fan of chaperoning dances because my whole teaching day sometimes seems like a chaper-oned event, my fiancé and I decided that we could not miss witnessing this social climax of the school year. On our way out to be with friends for the evening, we stopped just in time to see the dance starting to pick up steam.

Before we arrived at the Prom, I wasn't sure if making an appearance would be a good idea or not, but once we were there, I was glad we did. It was fun to see all of my students dressed to the nines and having a good time. I wasn't there more than five minutes when I was spotted by a core group of female music students, and I became the finish line for a sprint. They all took turns giving me a hug and I told each one in turn how beautiful they looked. The girls' professionally styled hair, make-up, and elegant sparkling dresses; the guys' tuxedos, although mostly un-tucked and missing jackets and bow ties by this hour, made them all look so grown up. Everyone gave off such a different image than they did sitting in my classroom...it is difficult to describe. I encourage you to make the time and effort to go to at least one school dance per year. Your kids will appreciate seeing you there, and you may gain some valuable insights into the many other facets of your students' lives.

April 30

Back to school after a beautiful and busy weekend. At least I feel a little more grounded than I did last week at this time—coming back from Easter break and feeling overwhelmed. Today was "Senior Appreciation Day," which

I guess is the official Senior skip day. It was both good and bad—some of the attitudes were absent, so I actually enjoyed Show Choir, but we didn't have some of the better talent either, so it made Concert Band a little tougher. It made me wonder what some of my groups will be like next year as different students come and go.

I had a great talk with Dr. V. today, just kinda touching base on everything. We discussed things from looking to hire the new choir director for next year to life in general. I told her a little bit about keeping these journals and wanting to turn them into a book someday and it was really neat to see how excited and happy she was! She is such a great fan of mine and that feels really good.

So, with emotions flying high and upcoming events swirling around you, we leave April. If you thought the weather was nice this past month, the coming weeks will be more so. If you thought the kids were tough to focus in April, brace yourself for more. However, if you thought that the past month was rewarding, educational, and touching for you as a teacher, there will be more of that to come as well. Congratulations as you reach the home stretch!

May

More than likely, your teaching obligations will extend at least a few days into June, but for most intents and purposes, May is the last full month of the school year. There are spring concerts, banquets, end of the year ceremonies, and graduations. There are also grades, paperwork, and planning for next year. Mentally, there is the knowledge that the year is almost over. You have "made it through" your first year of teaching. The cycle of students will continue, yet you have remained steadfast. But what has been changed by your presence and efforts? Whose lives have you impacted for the better? For me, May was a very emotional month where many of these thoughts and feelings raged in my mind. However, it was also a month in which I felt very proud of myself and my students for the many things we accomplished throughout the entire school year.

May 1

Today definitely had its ups and downs. Had a great rehearsal first hour with the Chamber Music Ensemble, then third hour with the Concert Choir was horrible. No one was listening; they were throwing paper around and behaving like children. It was really tough. I was almost to the point of

---

saying that I wasn't going to allow them to perform in the spring concert. Instead, after class I went into my office, sat down, and heaved a big sigh. Then I got back up and faced my next hour class, Jazz Band, which was wonderful. Sometimes it is really hard to deal with the peaks and valleys in teaching, many of which can happen in the course of just one day. The ups and downs really take a toll on me; how do I deal with them better? How do I not let them make me crazy?

I don't think I have a fool proof answer to that. I try to always be prepared for the classes I teach through good lesson plans and forward thinking, but it seems you can never truly plan 100 percent for kids and their attitudes and quirks from day to day. More than likely you have discovered this as well. Maybe we just need to worry less; to not take the ups and downs so seriously. It is a tough thing to do, since we care so much about music and teaching it to children. But we need to remember that even though we may not have taught the most successful lesson, something good can come of that. The experience gives us as teachers the opportunity to grow, both emotionally and professionally, and try new things.

Another "up" happened at the end of the day. After school, a girl from the Chorus came in to ask me for help on a solo she was working on. She did really well and was appreciative of my help. Then we started talking about college and her desire to be involved in music for the rest of her life. It was fun talking to her about her thoughts, giving her advice and telling her I would always be available to assist her. It was a neat experience to close such a roller coaster day.

May 2 – Wednesday

While Monday was the official "Senior Skip Day," today was the "Junior Day of Reflection," a sort of all-day retreat for the eleventh graders. While these days are nice for the kids and for the teachers who only teach one grade level, it really stinks for me because every one of my classes is a mixture of more than one grade level. So for the last two A days, I haven't had full rehearsals. It's tough to get a lot of things done with so many people gone, especially with a week and a half left before a concert. I appreciate the value of these events to the students, but it doesn't make my job easier, or rehearsals easier for the rest of the students in class.

Show Choir was very interesting today with only the Sophomores and Seniors there—they convinced me not to have a

> rehearsal, so we all talked instead. I
> enjoyed it; however, the Seniors were ask-
> ing me about the house and if my fiancé and
> I lived together. I really didn't know what to
> say...I ended up telling them the truth; that
> we did live together. But I also said that I
> trusted them to please not spread that
> knowledge around. What should I have
> done...lied? I helped them to move onto
> other subjects quickly, so that made me a
> little more comfortable. The point is that I
> really liked talking to them about regular
> everyday stuff. I wish I could do that more
> often, but how would I balance that with
> class time? I'm going to try and figure that
> out better because it made me feel good to
> be in those conversations with them.

It probably was not the smartest thing in the world for me to answer questions about my personal life with a group of students. Fortunately, nothing more came of the situation. But considering the fact that I teach at a religious school, I was treading on dangerous territory. On the other hand, I was not comfortable lying to them: kids can see through that. Part of me saw these kids as young adults, curious about how another young adult was dealing with being engaged and having a professional career. Maybe they saw themselves facing the same things in five years and wanted to know what lie ahead. So in a way, perhaps I was being a teacher in another regard, using my own life experiences to give them information.

However, worst case scenario: a parent hears that you are discussing your lifestyle choices with their son or daughter during class time, and they don't approve. They report it to the principal and demand you be reprimanded or even fired. I don't think I have to take you any further. Use extreme caution and sound judgment if you find yourself in this type of situation.

May 3

Today was an all-school "big recess." That means all the students and faculty have the same lunch period and some outside free time together to play sports, etc. It was fun for me because I got to talk to a lot of teachers during this time—something I don't usually get to do at lunch time.

Sometimes I allow students to eat down in the music room on all-school lunch days and I supervise. But before school this morning, boys who aren't even in music were in the room with other music students. They spilled some juice on the floor and left it for me to clean up. So I decided, as a consequence, that no one would be allowed to eat in there today. I told various students about it throughout the morning, so when the time for the "big recess" came, I locked the room up and left.

Part of me felt bad, but people have to know I am serious about the music department being respected. It was the same story after school: students were throwing mallets around, talking so loud they were almost screaming, and generally being idiots. I came out of my office and yelled at them, saying one more incident like this and they wouldn't be allowed in the room at any time except for class time. I told them I was sick and tired of their 5-year old behavior and they would suffer the consequences if it continued. They settled down quickly. I hate being the "bad guy." But in the long run, I see it as defending the respect of the music department.

I also see it as teaching kids some common decency and manners. Sometimes they just don't think: don't be afraid to let them know when they're being jerks.

May 4

Friday of a long week. But it was not as productive as a long week should seemingly be. I didn't have full rehearsals in hardly any of my A day classes all week with all the field trips, retreats, testing, and other activities going on. Next week won't be any better, either—more of the same. For some teachers it's great: if you teach a Junior math class and all the Juniors are gone, you get a free period.

Been trying hard to still be productive and make progress, do sectional work, etc., but most times it's not as ideal as a full rehearsal with all the kids present. Did some sight-reading of a piece for graduation with the Concert Band today. We've been rehearsing the same two pieces for like two weeks for the combined spring concert, so throwing the variety in there helps. Even though the concert pieces aren't perfect yet, I think they needed something new and different.

Variety is indeed the spice of life. In my experience, if you focus too much on one thing, whether it be a piece of music or a certain concept, oftentimes students will tune out. Yes, they may very well need to fully learn the "thing" you have been trying to teach them. But often a "break" from that very thing you are instructing gives the concept space to grow in the students' minds. Have you ever wracked your brain to remember someone's name, and as soon as you started thinking about something else, it suddenly came to you? Think about it....

May 7 - Monday

Last week to prepare for my last concert of the year. And like I thought last week, it's not going to be easy with all the field trips and other distractions going on this week. I know these things are important to their well-rounded education, but it's tough to put a concert together because of them. Busy writing concert notes and designing the program.

The best part of the day today was that the new choir director signed her contract for next year! It's official! I was in the main office dropping off some papers and saw Dr. V. and Mrs. W., the vocal director we hired to help with the musical earlier in the year. When Dr. V. invited me to walk over to them and told me the news, I just about started crying because I was so relieved! It's a weird feeling to know there is an end in sight to some of the craziness; to know that next year I will be able to specialize and focus, thus helping the kids learn better. Plus I'll actually "know the ropes" because my first year will be under my belt.

I don't mean to be the bearer of bad news, but all of your problems will not magically go away merely because you aren't a first-year teacher anymore. Granted, some things are more comfortable, such as knowing most of the faculty, doing budgets, and organizing concerts. But I remember my disappointment and frustration well into my second year of teaching because my trumpet section still talked too much, because I was still exhausted at the end of the day, or because the program still hadn't tripled in numbers. At first, I thought this made me a bad teacher—why hadn't I changed the world already? Many problems you face as a teacher are external, life long, uncontrollable, and do not change much from year to year. What you can change and control is your own attitude and reaction to your various challenges.

I am an idealist; I admit it without shame. I'm sure many of you are as well. You want every child to be motivated, every parent to always be pleased, every teacher to like you, and every concert to be performed flawlessly. This will not happen your second year of teaching...or your fifty-second year of teaching. This realization does not change my idealistic nature, but perhaps someday it will give me the permission I need to not be so hard on myself. I'm working on it....

May 9

In-service day and presentation time for myself and the other Fine Arts teachers. This year at in-service meetings, each department had to do a presentation for the rest of the faculty about their classes and curriculum, and this was our month. I was very nervous—more so than I had planned on. Here I am, a first-year teacher having to speak in front of the whole faculty! While at the same time trying to promote and "sell" what I do! I enjoyed the actual

---

preparing and planning of the speech, but as I waited for it to be my turn to speak, I got more and more nervous. When the moment arrived, however, all my fears evaporated and I had a great time delivering my information. I even played saxophone for the group; one time without dynamics or feeling, the second time to show how I teach musicianship and aesthetics in my classes. They clapped when I was done and seemed to enjoy it—I got lots of great compliments and Dr. V. gave me a hug later in the day! She again said how proud she was of me; she is always so supportive.

The actual school day after the in-service was good as well. I was feeling pretty upbeat and confident after the successful presentation. For the first time today, I played along with the Jazz Band. I did it because the first also sax player was gone, so I covered his part...but I think in the future I will do it more often even if everyone is present. It was fun! More importantly, it brought me closer to what the students were doing—phrasing, accenting, etc. with them.

Being a leader from the podium is important. As you teach a piece of music to a group of students, you need to help them set a tempo, keep a steady beat, and work on balance, blend, intonation, and rhythms just to name a few. But there are times when playing or singing along with students only strengthens your instruction and leadership. Student musicians need good models, so this is one way to accomplish that. In my experience, I would not play with students every rehearsal—they may not practice as much and could begin to rely on following you without learning the music themselves. But in general, playing or singing along with an ensemble is a very valuable instructional tool.

May 10

Thursday—and the last day I will rehearse with my A day groups before our concert on Sunday. It makes me a little nervous because it seems like such a long time between now and then. I think they will be okay, though.

I really had a tough time with a girl in Concert Band today. She was purposely being disruptive and hurtful...not to another student, but to me. For example, I was making announcements at the beginning of class, one of which was the fact that I was disappointed in their attendance at sectionals earlier today. This student sarcastically said "Darn!" and snapped her fingers together. It might not seem like a big thing, but it hurt my feelings. I'm not sure what I did to deserve her attitude, but I did my best to ignore it, even though inside it felt like someone was stepping on my chest.

Then, as we got into rehearsal, I completely surprised her: I complimented her

---

> playing. She was playing a certain part very
> musically and I gave her genuine praise for
> it. She looked at me strangely at first, like
> she didn't know whether to believe me or
> not, then took the compliment well. I hope
> she feels bad for being such a jerk towards
> me beforehand.

It may be tempting to engage in petty behavioral wars with students when they do not treat you with respect or kindness. The key here is to be the bigger and better person when they are being rotten. Not only are you not stooping to their level, but you are also showing them and any other students paying attention what kind of adult you are…and modeling that behavior for them to (hopefully) emulate.

> **May 11**
>
> Friday—and it feels like it, too. But my B day groups rehearsed well today, especially the Concert Choir. I don't know what it is about my choral groups in general, but it's like they never worry about rehearsing seriously until the last minute. We stood in a circle today so the kids could really listen to each other's parts. I got them to chime in as far as comments and critiquing also. Jazz Band and Chamber Music also did well and should sound great on Sunday.

I did a fun activity in Music Fundamentals today. I gave each student a sheet of paper with a Romantic era piece of music written on it: "In the Hall of the Mountain King," "Carnival of the Animals," etc. I then played a recording of each piece for them and they tried to guess which piece was which based only on the sound of the music. They liked it, and it tied in well with the idea of program music we are starting in our Romantic music history unit.

May 14

The day after the last big concert of the year—the Spring Mother's Day Concert. Just like the Christmas Concert, it was a combined performance, so all of the vocal and instrumental groups showed off their talents. Each group performed two or three pieces.

I had been worried about this concert for a while, at least for the three weeks since we returned from Easter break. Not only about how well the students would do, but how the concert would be received by the parents being scheduled on Mother's Day and how I personally would do on my last concert of the year. What would everyone think, now that a year of concerts has passed? How would I feel about the progress of the department? How would I feel in general? The answers are wonderful, good, and exhausting...maybe not necessarily in that order...I did literally collapse when I got home yesterday after the concert—my energy was completely spent. But I received lots of great compliments and felt pretty good about most of the performances. I always feel like things could be a little better, but I try not to let it get me down and ruin the rest of my proud feelings about the concert.

Even though I gave most groups some free time during class today (except for Concert Band—rehearsing for graduation), it still seemed like a busy day. Some students and I sold roses around school today that were left over from the ones we sold at yesterday's concert. Plus I was busy preparing what I was going to present at the all-school awards night tonight and getting ready for the Senior Recital tomorrow night. These couple days just feel like constant activity.

At first I thought my presentation at the all-school awards night was merely an obligation I had to fulfill. But when I was actually in the act of speaking to the student body and their parents and giving out the music department's major yearly achievement awards, it was a very special experience that I was delighted to be a part of. I was promoting the music department to the entire school by describing the students' various achievements. I experienced the privilege of seeing students receive awards and be happy and proud of themselves, with pleased parents looking on. I got the chance to reward and thank some of my best, brightest, and most talented students.

After the ceremony, one of my students to whom I presented an award wanted his father to take a picture of me with him, which was an amazing feeling. I felt important and special, like I had really made a difference in this student's life. He told me the awards and recognition meant a lot to him; in turn, that meant a lot to me. What an amazing thing to be a part of!

Now we head back down the roller coaster. After the award ceremony, several parents came in to school to help sort the flower bulb order which came in that day (Remember a few months ago—selling these as a band fundraiser? Now it was time for delivery…). I was glad for the parents' assistance, but I wasn't happy to spend another two hours of my evening at school. And of course, some parts of the order weren't correct. We were missing several items from certain people's orders; some bulbs were substituted for others that apparently hadn't yielded a good crop. A few parents agreed to contact the company and find out how to get our missing orders, so I was glad I didn't have to add that to my busy schedule.

There's really no way to avoid fundraisers. I simply tell you the above facts to inform you of the time and energy they consume. Even if you have a wonderful parent support group as I did, a lot of the work and worry will still fall on your shoulders. Be prepared and keep a positive attitude; it will hopefully influence your students and parents to do the same.

May 15

Lots of different things happened today—in order of the day: First hour, the Chamber music kids still can't play the arrangement of "Flight of the Bumble Bee" we've been working on for months. Were my expectations too high? I mean, it's a tough piece, but that's why I gave them a long time to work on it. I'm really disturbed about it. Second hour a couple of students and I started getting the theatre organized for the Senior Recital tonight. Third hour I gave the Concert Choir an off day because of the concert on Sunday. Then I felt like a jerk because a parent visitor came in with someone from the guidance department in hopes of seeing a rehearsal. This parent was checking out the school for her eighth grade daughter and I'm not sure how much I actually impressed her.

Next hour, the Jazz Band was fun—we brought out some charts they played last year to add to our Fine Arts Day performance. They were having fun playing old tunes they were already familiar with and I enjoyed watching them count off pieces by themselves, etc. During Fundamentals class, I heard good presentations from the Seniors in that class for their final project (this week is finals week for the Seniors, so they are done earlier than the rest of the school).

The Senior Recital was something new and different, and its debut was in the school auditorium that evening. It was my idea to start this new tradition because we had a Senior Recital every year at my high school. I think it is a very special and appropriate way to showcase the Senior musicians one last time before graduation.

I had spread the word and asked which Seniors wanted to be a part of the recital for about a month, so they had time to prepare. Some wanted to do a solo, others chose to perform a duet with another classmate. There ended up being about ten students who wanted to participate: a good number for the inaugural recital. I made the programs, hung posters around school, and generally tried to promote the new event. This is important, especially with new events—most times they need help catching on. Be proactive!

The actual recital that evening was a success; at least I saw it that way. Our audience was pretty small—maybe a couple dozen people at most. But I think as the tradition continues, the fan club will grow. More importantly, Senior students had their own avenue in which to perform, and they did so beautifully. What a great opportunity for a young adult: to be on a stage, doing something they love. Many may not ever have that chance again, so I was glad to help facilitate this performance.

Another joyous occasion during the month of May was the music department banquet. Unlike the Senior recital, this tradition was already in place. Similar to sports banquets, the idea of the music department banquet is to present awards, such as solo and ensemble medals, talk about each groups' successes throughout the year, and generally get all music students and their parents together to have a good time. With the help of the music parents group, I reserved a banquet room in a local university union, picked the menu, wrote and sent information letters and sign-up sheets to all the music department families, and collected money for the event. I encourage you to begin this process six to eight weeks before you want the banquet to take place—this way you'll have plenty of time to organize the above steps.

After all of the planning, the night of the banquet finally arrived. I was excited to share a good time and my congratulations with music students and their families; however, I was also nervous about speaking in front of them at such an event. I don't know why—all I had been doing all year was talking to large crowds at concerts and school assemblies, plus I knew all the students and almost all of their parents! Perhaps my anxiety came from wanting to make the event special for everyone…and not screwing up and saying someone's name wrong or something…But in the end, everything went well. The smiles on students' faces on their way up to me at the podium when I called their name to receive an award were priceless, as they were for the few upperclassmen on the all-school awards night. The applause for my students and I and our achievements was eternally valuable. I really enjoyed myself and think that most of the parents, relatives, and students did as well. It is important to celebrate the success of an organization in this fashion at the end of the school year.

Allow me to briefly discuss general housekeeping items in order to make your banquet run as smoothly as possible. I suggest making notes for yourself: an outline of things you want to say and/or a general order of the festivities. Perhaps you want everyone to eat dinner first, then you wish to announce large group awards, such as festival ratings, and lastly present individual awards. Maybe you have an entirely different format, but whatever the order of events for the evening, make them clear and easy to follow so people know what to expect. If you have the time and energy (ha!), you may even want to design and print programs for the occasion. Dress up, and be excited and positive—your demeanor sets the tone of importance and priority. Lastly, give out as many awards as you possibly can—nothing is worse for a child than to sit at a function such as this and watch everyone else be recognized. Even undeserving kids? Of course not. But consider some small token for your better students who may not have gone to a competition or earned an individual medal or "letter," such as a certificate of achievement or a pin. If a student feels good, happy, and successful around you and your program, they will keep enrolling in your classes and building your ensembles.

May 21

   I took a personal day on Friday to be
with my mom and my sister—they came to
town and we went wedding dress shopping!
It was a nice day, but both it and the entire
weekend went way too fast. Now it is
Monday and I feel like I'm way behind again.
Now that the Seniors are gone and my class
sizes and talents have diminished, it makes
rehearsing more difficult. Coupled with the
end of the school year apathy and restless-
ness, I wonder sometimes if I am really
accomplishing anything with solid musical or
educational value.
   As the end of the year approaches, I
wonder how much of a difference I have
really made: how many lives have I really
touched? To top off all of these feelings,
there was a two and a half hour band parent
meeting tonight that could have been done
in a hour. I love their help and I couldn't do
certain things without them, but sometimes
I feel like it's just overload. I feel like all
the things they talk about are just more
things for me to get stressed out over.

May 22

   I thought I would really like the end of
the school year, but so far I hate it. With

the last spring concert over, some groups don't have any major performances to prepare for, so I feel like we're kinda treading water. That doesn't make me feel like a great teacher— wasting time or learning opportunities. I'm glad I scheduled the spring concert later next year. I mean, I told the kids the last spring concert was their final and I feel there is definitely merit in that, but there's so much more time to learn more things and now they're not motivated. Glad that the Jazz Band, Concert Band, Show Choir, etc. still have performances: graduation, fine arts night, etc. to keep them working.

Am I in the "real world?" I never thought school was the real world when I was in it as a student. I couldn't wait to be a grown up out in the "real world." Is school as a teacher different? I feel I'm doing something that enriches people and makes a difference, or at least trying. The apathy and the blank stares, the zoning out, the not paying attention or not giving your best effort: that's what gets me down, even as I walk by classes that aren't my own and see it. The way I see it, this apathy is the death of progress, the enemy of energy. I know I was like this sometimes when I was in high school, but I can't take it from the other side.

I hate the "tedious" parts of teaching— telling kids to be quiet all the time, to behave, to respect property, etc. I hate what seems to be wasted time, wasted effort, and wasted worry.

> The school's president puts out a monthly newsletter about the happenings in the entire school. With all the great things occurring in the music department, such as concerts and musicians' successful ratings from the state competition, I thought surely there would be a mention of them, but not a word. Sports, of course, but no fine arts. Sometimes I think I'm just tired of fighting the battle—does nothing I do make a difference?
>
> I've gotten all these compliments as a first year teacher about how well I presented awards or how great the concert was or this or that. Why don't I feel like I'm doing a good job? Why don't I feel successful? Why do I feel unhappy and stressed? Is this only end of the year junk, or are there deeper problems and unrest within myself?

At the end of the school year, you may experience some of these same feelings. Everything gets on your nerves and you start asking yourself questions like:

"Have I done enough this year?"

"Have I covered enough?"

"Have the kids learned and experienced enough?"

"What is 'enough,' anyway?"

Like you may be, I was, and still am at times so frightened of being just average or mediocre. I am so scared that I'm not making a difference to anyone. One of the many reasons I wanted to be a music teacher was to spread the knowledge, passion, and power that music can have with young people and make a difference in their lives. A difference for the better. A difference toward the inspired. When the school year is coming to an end, teachers have fewer and fewer chances to leave that mark. As the days in May went by, instead of feeling more and more happy or relieved, I was doubting my abilities and my effectiveness for the entire year.

At a certain mental level, I knew these thoughts and feelings were illogical and unfounded. You probably do as well, but that still does not help us feel better. Why do we feel like such failures when we should be celebrating our successes?

I think that all too often we rely on external circumstances to make us feel happy and successful. This is not altogether a bad thing; it is human nature. Our team wins a game, a concert goes well, a child smiles, or we receive a compliment, and we feel good. But what happens when the boss does not recognize our hard work, the kids behave poorly, or a performance does not run as we hoped it would? Most of us tumble into a state of despair and disappointment. We worked ourselves to the bone and put our whole being into doing something well and it didn't go absolutely perfectly. We feel awful and blame ourselves for circumstances which are most often out of our control. How productive is all of this?

My challenge to you is this—and believe me, it is a challenge. Focus on the positive. We have been told this our entire lives, but when it comes to putting it into practice, many of us act as though it is an alien concept. It is easy to become overrun with the things that aren't right or perfect. Instead, let us all try to appreciate the things that are. Maybe the school president didn't acknowledge the good works of the music department when I thought he should have, but that doesn't take away the fact that there are indeed good works to talk about. Maybe there are some bratty, insensitive students in your school, but that shouldn't take away from the awesome, thoughtful, talented, and special kids who are there as well.

I have something that may help you carry this concept out to its fullest. From my very first days and weeks as a young teacher, I would tape positive things I received up on my office walls. When the marching band made the local newspaper, I cut out the article and up it went. When students gave me their Senior pictures or snapshots their parents took at a concert; when I received cards on Valentine's Day; when I got thank you letters for the letters of recommendation I wrote...they all went up on what came to be know as "Ms. B's wall." Even though I have not been teaching an incredibly long time, I currently have an area of about thirty square feet wallpapered with my beloved mementos, and it seems to grow every week. I look at these things every day and they bring out the best in me. They remind me of the good things I've done. They remind me that I have done enough. They remind me that maybe...just maybe.... I have indeed made a difference.

May 24

Well, today was definitely the kind of day I needed to turn the week and my depressed feelings around. Today was Grandparent's Day and classes were shortened so the school could have a church service and reception for the grandparents and their student grandchildren. The String Ensemble played during the service and also later at the reception in the cafeteria, and they were absolutely beautiful! It was really a fun experience—it was less pressure than a concert and the kids seemed to enjoy themselves. At the reception, people were walking by us, smiling and obviously enjoying the music: that only enhances our own enjoyment.

To continue the festivities, tonight was Fine Arts Night, a night where the Art Department turns much of the school into an art gallery to showcase student work from throughout the year. The Jazz Band and Chamber Ensemble provided some background music at the event. It was such a new and relaxed environment for us to perform in. We played pieces we had already performed during the year, or as in the Jazz Band's case, even resurrected tunes from last year. The kids really had fun and people who didn't normally hear us or come to our concerts had the opportunity to listen to our efforts. I had fun too, and it was a great feeling to have after a few days of doubt.

May 29

    Today was the Baccalaureate Mass for the graduating Seniors. It lasted about two hours and was scheduled in the middle of the school day so the whole school could be a part of the event. Most of my energy was spent getting set up and warmed up for the musical performances at the Mass itself. I guess in the past when the music program was really struggling, they wouldn't even have live music playing at the Mass or even for the graduation ceremony—they would play a recording. So, while I feel nervous about sounding nice for the graduates and their families, I am also proud just to be part of the event—that I have helped the program to grow.

    It feels weird to have been a teacher here for almost a full school year now and to still be going through things for the first time, like this Baccalaureate ceremony. I was worried the whole service if I was doing things right and if everything would work out.

Of course, everything worked out fine. My principal was supportive as usual and the music helped the ceremony flow nicely. Even as we get to be seasoned professionals, I think many of us still worry about doing things "right" when there really isn't a "right" or "wrong." Instead, it's how things were done in the past and how to do things differently. And oftentimes, different and new are just fine. Usually, anything can come together and make sense if you are prepared and flexible.

May 30 – Graduation

"Okay, this is our last performance of the year, let's make it a great one," I said to the Concert Band and Show Choir as we warmed up for the performance at our high school graduation ceremony. We performed "Pomp and Circumstance," the National Anthem, and a recessional march. Although wonderful for parents and graduating Seniors, many people may think it was just another performance for me and the ensembles: that it all was pretty standard and typical....

But it was not. The seventeen and eighteen year olds weren't the only ones to graduate. I graduated that night, too. I survived my first year of teaching. In fact, I did more than survive...I planned. I organized. I inspired. I listened.

I taught.

Conclusion

So, you've made it—congratulations! As you now know first-hand, education has to be one of the toughest professions out there. But hopefully also one of the most rewarding. My hope for you is that you had at least as many fulfilling moments as you did challenging ones during your first year of teaching. Think back...I bet you did (all those "little" things count, too).

But the reality is that teaching is too difficult, too time-consuming, or too emotionally draining for some people to handle. Will you continue teaching? Will you be a lifelong teacher? Will I?

The truth is, I don't know. Some days I feel as though I can't handle another minute surrounded by teenage music students. Other times I can't imagine not being part of their lives. What I do know is this: as a teacher, I have had moments of extreme joy and fulfillment. The kind of joy and fulfillment one can only receive by teaching something to a child, helping someone become a better person, making a difference in a life, or changing things for the good of the world. However, don't be too surprised when you discover that one of the lives you change and "make a difference" in may just be your own....

Please enjoy a journal entry from my second year of teaching. I reflect on this day often, because it reminds me of what teaching is really all about....

October 11

Little did I know when I woke up this morning what a special day I was in store for. My first classes and lessons passed in a fairly normal fashion, and about halfway through the day I was outside on the practice field with the Marching Band. It was a beautiful autumn day, with sunshine and crisp, cool air. We were putting some finishing touches on our show for the big Homecoming game tomorrow night.

From my vantage point on the podium, I saw what appeared to be a student standing on the far end of the field, observing our rehearsal. At first, I really didn't pay attention to him: I assumed it was perhaps one of the Color Guard's boyfriends skipping out of lunch so he could watch them practice. However, about five minutes later, the whole Color Guard screamed, ran over to this individual, and practically tackled him with hugs. From my far distance away, I still didn't know who this person was or what the big fuss was about. Luckily, the class period was almost over— the concentration level of most of my students was now thrown by the wayside because of this commotion.

I dismissed the Band, and we began to walk off the field in the direction of the popular stranger. As I got closer, I realized this was no stranger at all, but "Nate," my most talented Senior from last school year. He was now attending a top music university on a full scholarship because of his brilliance on his instrument. Back home for fall break, he was paying a visit to the school. I greeted him warmly and walked back into the building with him and some of my current students, listening to his "freshmen" tales of bad roommates, worse food, and college classes.

I thought the main reason Nate dropped by was to see his younger friends, but as the moment unfolded, it turned out he was more interested in speaking with me. He would never say this out loud because of his shy nature, but the fact started becoming apparent to me as his friends left the music room to go to lunch or other classes and he remained, clearly in no rush to go anywhere else. Soon, it was just the two of us, and as we stood in the middle of the band room, he told me something I'll never forget.

"Ms. B., you know theory class from last year...well, it's helped me a lot this year. I'm way ahead of the other people 'cause it's all like review for me. You really helped me out a lot."

I don't remember my response—probably some inadequate, embarrassed smile and incoherent babble, but I do remember how his words made me feel. To a non-teacher or the average passerby, this comment may go under-appreciated. But to me, someone might as well have told me that I was the most wonderful person to ever live. My heart felt like it was soaring and my head cleared, as though some of the crisp autumn air from earlier in the day had finally gotten into my soul. That dear young man probably has no idea how important and special his small showing of gratitude was, and still is, to me. But knowing that I have made a difference and helped even one person gives me the strength to face another day. Maybe I will find a way to reach another student someday. It is entirely possible: I am a music teacher.

Reference Section

As one of my fellow teachers in our school's English department likes to say, "We all benefit from stealing from each other!" What she means is that teachers help each other immensely by sharing information such as lesson plans, strategies, or grading scales. In fact, in our school's copy room, there is a whole file of tests, rubrics, and project ideas on a variety of subject matters. While I don't believe people "copy" anything directly, it is a wonderful resource—an avenue in which to share ideas. One of the biggest mistakes I believe we often make as teachers is thinking we have to accomplish everything by ourselves. Utilize your co-workers and let them utilize you. You are not alone.

The following pages are by no means an all-inclusive package of everything you will ever need as a music teacher, but hopefully my examples will give you some ideas on how to enrich or improve your own teaching strategies. As my English teacher friend would say, "Steal them!" I won't mind.

Instrumental Music Handbook

M _____ *Director of Instrumental Music*
000 E. Pine Ave.
Springfield, WI 53123
(123) 000-0000 ex. 00

This handbook contains valid information for the following performance-based classes:

> **Concert Band** *(including marching band and pep band responsibilities)*
> **Jazz Band**
> **String Ensemble**
> **Chamber Music Ensemble**

Our Mission:

To create fabulous instrumental music while growing as musicians both individually and through our ensembles and maintaining a positive, respectful, efficient and family-based atmosphere.

In order to reach this Goal:

It is expected that every student in a performance-based class **practice at least___hour (s) five times a week, outside of school rehearsals.** Consider this your "homework" for your respective music class. I will not require documentation of this practice—it is "on your honor"—you are all mature, responsible musicians, and I will treat you as such. **You** are responsible for the success of your ensemble!

As musical ensembles that depend upon the strength of its members, we need **100% attendance at every concert and/or performance.** I am assuming that you are in a performing music class because you want to be and that you enjoy performing, so I hope that this will not be a problem. If a **major conflict** such as a family event or emergency arises that would permit you from performing at a required concert or event, please let me know as soon as possible. We will try to work out an alternative project to avoid a significant drop in your grade for the class.

Concert/Performance Dress Requirements

The following formal dress is required of you at every performance:

Concert Band
Band uniform: marching uniform or concert dress tuxedo, depending upon the performance *(pep band rugbys for pep band)*

String Ensemble and Chamber Music Ensemble
Men: black dress pants, black socks and black dress shoes, white dress shirt with a black tie *(black suit jacket optional)*

Women: black dress *(no "spaghetti" sleeves and length below the knee),* or a black skirt with length below the knee with a white dress blouse, or black dress pants with a white dress blouse—all above choices with black socks or pantyhose and black dress shoes

Jazz Band
A more "flashy" version of the above will be discussed: i.e. perhaps adding hats, colorful ties, etc.

> *"Image" counts for a lot—your audience will see you before they will hear you. Please help your group display the sharpest, best image possible. Thanks!*

Rehearsal/Classroom Policies
The "biggie" in the music department is **respect.** If you are doing something that doesn't fall under that concept, then you are probably not doing what is best for you or your ensemble. For those of you who need a list:

1. Please do not talk while others are talking or rehearsing.
2. Come prepared! Practice outside of class time and bring your music, a pencil, your instrument, and anything else you need to every rehearsal!
3. Be in your seat, quiet and ready to begin class at the specified time—you will receive about 3 minutes beyond the bell ringing to get your instruments out and be settled in your places in order to begin class efficiently.

4. Keep the music room clean and treat instruments and property appropriately.
5. An obvious lack of effort or negative attitude will not be tolerated.

I expect that you will want your ensemble to be the best that it can be; therefore, I will leave the majority of these classroom policies up to you to enforce. Be a positive role model to others! Remind them of our goals! Is their behavior helping us to achieve our goals? If I have to step in, I will give you the following:

1. Reminder (no points off your grade)
2. Warning (2 points off your participation grade for the day)
3. 2nd warning (4 points off your participation grade for the day)
4. Outside action (detentions, demerits, etc.)

Course Assessments and Grading

All of the above classes are performance-based, meaning that the majority of our time, effort and grading will be based on participation in concerts, rehearsals, (lessons and sectionals for certain groups) and personal practice. If our mission is to become better musicians, these are essential. Every quarter should show improvements, both on the part of the individual and the ensemble.

Point values to be earned
20 points per rehearsal/lesson/sectional
100 points per concert/performance

Other important concepts in our ensembles, *and in life,* are **positive attitudes, working hard, respecting others and property, punctuality, and teamwork.** These ideas and how well you execute them will be a factor in your grade, as well as your attention to the above classroom policies. Please see the rubric at the end of this handbook for the specific instrumental music department standards and how they will be assessed.

How to get an "A":
Energetic participation at all performances, as well as proper

dress at concerts
Attendance at lessons and sectionals
Hard work in class
Practice outside of class
Good attitude and respect toward others

Lessons

Individual and group music lessons and sectionals will also
be a consideration in earning a grade in certain music classes.
This smaller, more personalized rehearsal atmosphere is
critical in helping both you and your various ensembles
improve in musical ability.

Concert Band members will participate in individual lessons.
These will be scheduled during the student's study halls,
class studies, or before or after school for a duration
of about 15 minutes on a bi-weekly basis. These sectionals and lessons will be part of your grade. The exact
schedule and its rotation will be finalized when the
school year starts.

The Music Letter

A great reward for a job well done and a show of pride in
the music department is the *Music Letter.* Very similar to
the letters given out for sports or academics, the music
letter is an honorable award given at the end of the school
year to candidates who have demonstrated exceptional abilities in the three main categories of musicianship, leadership
and service.

Specifics to be considered

Perfect attendance at performances

Participation in solo and ensemble festival

Participation in the musical

Volunteer work for the music department

Upperclassman status

*Color guard from the marching band can be eligible to earn
a letter after 3 years of participation.*

Last words

Each different ensemble, along with this handbook, received a "flyer" with its group's specific performance dates for the fall/winter semester, and will receive one for the spring later in the year. When you receive it, please post the flyer on the fridge at home or somewhere else where it reminds you of what we are doing in the *Department of Instrumental Music!*

If you have any questions or concerns about anything, please give me a call at school _____ . If I left something out or did not make something clear, please let me know!

Thank you so much and I'm looking forward to a great year!

M _____

This is an example of a 'flyer' that I make for all ensembles so they are aware of their performance obligations.

Pep Band Performances
Winter 2002/2003
Basketball and Hockey

Fri., Dec. 6—Girls vs. Arrowhead *(home opener!)*—6:45

Fri., Dec. 13—Boys vs. South *(home opener!)*—6:45

Fri., Jan. 3—Boys vs. North—6:45

Sat., Jan. 11—Hockey vs. Arrowhead—8:15—Eble

Sat., Jan. 18—Hockey vs. East—8:15—Eble

Tues., Jan. 21—Girls vs. Lutheran—6:45

All basketball games are at the school gym—the 6:45/8:15 time above is when you need to arrive at either school or Eble Ice Arena on Bluemound Road—the actual game time is 7:30 for basketball dates and 8:45 for hockey.

These Performances are Required!

Every Student Is a Vital Part of Our Band!

Mark Your Calendars Now!!!

Bonding Games

The Knot Game: Put students in groups of no less than six. Have them stand in a tight circle facing each other, extend their hands and grasp the hands of two different people across the circle. Untangle! They may duck down, step over each other, twist around, etc., but they must not break each other's grip. If certain groups finish before others, join two smaller groups together for a 'master knot.' Appropriate for many different ages.

The Trust Game: This one I would recommend for older middle school and high school students. Put students in groups of 7-8 and have them form a tight, shoulder-to-shoulder circle facing each other. One person starts in the middle of the circle, with everyone eventually getting a turn. The members of the outside circle put their hands out in front of them at chest level. The person inside the circle crosses their arms across their chest and allows him/herself to fall into the members of the circle. S/He 'trusts' the teammates to catch him/her and pass him/her gently on across the circle. It may take a little coaching and a lot of supervision— you as the teacher may even have to be the first 'victim,' but once it gets going, it is a neat team-building activity.

Name: _____

Chorus   Introduction to New Piece Project

1. Name of Piece: _____

2. How many sharps (#) or flats (b) in the key signature?

   That means the piece is in the key of: _____

3. Is this piece 2, 3, or 4 part harmony? _____

4. How many different time signatures are there? _____

   Name them: _____

5. What are the different dynamic levels *(louds and softs)* and
   where do they change? Ex., at measure 10 there is a *f* mark-
   ed, meaning we should sing louder.

6. In your opinion, in what measure lies the most difficult rhythm?
   Why?

7. In your opinion, what will be the most challenging part of working on this piece? Why?

8. In your opinion, what will be the most fun part of working on
   this piece? Why?

Presenter's Name:_____

Fundamentals of Music Quarter Project
Peer Evaluation

1. Rate the following areas of this student's presentation, one being the worst and ten being the best:

Informative: 10 9 8 7 6 5 4 3 2 1

Creative: 10 9 8 7 6 5 4 3 2 1

Easy to Follow: 10 9 8 7 6 5 4 3 2 1

Interesting: 10 9 8 7 6 5 4 3 2 1

Preparedness: 10 9 8 7 6 5 4 3 2 1

2. I learned the following from this presentation:

3. If I would have done this presentation, I would have done the following things differently:

4. If I was grading this presentation, it would receive a:
   A   B   C   D   F

Name:_____

University Band Festival Critique Form

One of the best things that a great band can do is listen to and learn from other bands!

Please answer the following questions related to the high school band you listened to.

1. Name of Ensemble:

2. Approximate # of members:

3. Names of pieces they performed:

4. Write a comment about each of the following concepts relative to this band:

Tone —
Balance/Blend —
Dynamics —
In tune —
Articulations —
Transitions —
Melody vs. Harmony —

Other elements —

5. What did you generally like the most about this group's performance?

6. What did you think needed the most improvement?

Instrumental Music Department

Lesson Progress Sheet

Name: _____ Instrument: _____

Major Scales
C: 1 Octave _____ Full Range _____
G: 1 Octave _____ Full Range _____
F: 1 Octave _____ Full Range _____
D: 1 Octave _____ Full Range _____
Bb: 1 Octave _____ Full Range _____
A: 1 Octave _____ Full Range _____
Eb: 1 Octave _____ Full Range _____
E: 1 Octave _____ Full Range _____
Ab: 1 Octave _____ Full Range _____
B: 1 Octave _____ Full Range _____
Db: 1 Octave _____ Full Range _____
Gb: 1 Octave _____ Full Range _____

Minor Scales (nat., harm., mel.)
a: 1 Octave _____ Full Range _____
e: 1 Octave _____ Full Range _____
d: 1 Octave _____ Full Range _____
b: 1 Octave _____ Full Range _____
g: 1 Octave _____ Full Range _____
f#: 1 Octave _____ Full Range _____
c: 1 Octave _____ Full Range _____
c#: 1 Octave _____ Full Range _____
f: 1 Octave _____ Full Range _____
g#: 1 Octave _____ Full Range _____
bb: 1 Octave _____ Full Range _____
eb: 1 Octave _____ Full Range _____

Chromatic Scale: 1 Octave: _____ Full Range: _____

Lesson Book/Etude Material/Band Music:

Solos/Other Liturature:

Name: _____

Performance Evaluation

Please answer these questions, using complete thoughts and sentences, *in relation to our concert.*

What did you like about the performance in general?
Your individual performance?

What can **you** improve on, not only thinking in terms of the past concert, but what can you do to be a better musician in the future? What are your goals as a vocalist/instrumentalist?

Do you think that any performance can be perfect?
If perfection is an impossible goal, what is our goal?

Do you feel connected to the music? To your fellow musicians? Why or why not?

How does music and performing make you feel? Why?
What feelings did you have during our performance?

What have you learned through our process of rehearsal and performance?

Any other thoughts or comments:

Uniform Checkout Form

Concert/Marching Band
1) Uniform Number: _____
   incl. tux shirt, pants, jacket,
   overlay, and garment bag

2) Hat Number and Size: ____

3) Please check the following items:
   Plume: _____
   Pair of Spats: _____
   Bow Tie: _____

Color Guard
1) Uniform Number: _____
2) Uniform Size: _____

I understand that the above items have been loaned to me by the Music Department. I will return all of the above items in good condition and in a timely fashion. I accept financial responsibility for any lost or damaged pieces of the uniform.

Print Name: _____   Phone: _____

Signature: _____   Date: _____

Uniform Checkout Form

Concert/Marching Band
1) Uniform Number: _____
   incl. tux shirt, pants, jacket,
   overlay, and garment bag

2) Hat Number and Size: ____

3) Please check the following items:
   Plume: _____
   Pair of Spats: _____
   Bow Tie: _____

Color Guard
1) Uniform Number: _____
2) Uniform Size: _____

I understand that the above items have been loaned to me by the Music Department. I will return all of the above items in good condition and in a timely fashion. I accept financial responsibility for any lost or damaged pieces of the uniform.

Print Name: _____   Phone: _____

Signature: _____   Date: _____

Daily Participation Rubric

	A	B
1	Musicianship	Strong attention to musical detail and quality. Open to explore new musical ideas. Pride in rehearsal and performance.
2	Technique	Strong facility of instrument, i.e. notes, positions, embouchure, fingerings, etc.
3	Group Effort	High level of attention and listening in rehearsal. Consistently positive attitude. Respect for others and property. Displays teamwork and encourages others.
4	Individual Effort	Personal practice is apparent. Evidence of continual growth and progress. Lesson and sectional attendance is perfect. High organizational skills.
5	Points Earned per Day and Performance	20-19 Exemplary

C	E	F
Attention to some musical details. Generally open to new challenges. Takes some pride in work.	Inconsistent or careless attention to musical details and quality of performance. Resistance to new musical ideas. Rarely displays musical pride.	No concern or awareness of musicality. Complete disregard for new challenges. No pride in rehearsal or performance.
Developing facility of instrument. Comfortable with most concepts. Several insecurities in playing instrument. Many key concepts are not known.	Several insecurities in playing instrument. Many key concepts are not known.	No apparent technique or competence on instrument.
Mostly attentive in rehearsal—talks rarely and listens frequently. Positive attitude in most situations. Respect for concept is fairly apparent. Developing idea of teamwork.	Not attentive in rehearsal. Talkative and disruptive. Positive attitude only some of the time. Episodes of disrespect. Resistance to teamwork on one or more occasions.	Low attention in rehearsal—several behavior concerns. Positive attitude is rare. Complete disrespect for individuals, group or property. Does not work well with others.
Working toward optimum practice time. Steady growth and progress. Few lessons or sectionals missed. Organized and prepared for class in most situations.	Infrequent practice or limited growth. Several lessons or sectionals missed. Rarely organized or prepared—relies on others for copies of music or materials.	No practice evident— little progress made. Extremely low attendance at sectionals or lessons. No effort to be prepared or organized for class.
18-17 Proficient	16-15 Average	14-0 Not Meeting Standard

Fundamentals of Music Presentation Rubric

1	Informative	I can tell this student really researched this topic. **Points: 20-18**
2	Creative	Student put much time and effort into making project special and creative. **Points: 20-18**
3	Easy to Follow	Student spoke clearly and presentation made sense. **Points: 20-18**
4	Interesting	Student made topic exciting and engaged the listener. **Points: 20-18**
5	Prepared	Student was very prepared for this presentation. **Points: 20-18**
6	Quiz	Quiz given was relevant to project and tied project together for other students. **Points: 20-18**

Student seems to be somewhat informed. **Points: 17-14**	Student lacks major information. **Points: 13 or below**
Student has some creative aspects included. **Points: 17-14**	Project contains no creative elements. **Points: 13 or below**
Presentation rambled at times. **Points: 17-14**	No organization apparent. **Points: 13 or below**
Presentation had some interesting moments. **Points: 17-14**	Even the presenter seemed bored. **Points: 13 or below**
Student seemed somewhat prepared. **Points: 17-14**	Student seemed to be unprepared. **Points: 13 or below**
Quiz was only semi-related or relevant to presentation. **Points: 17-14**	Quiz was displayed as an afterthought. **Points: 13 or below**

Teacher Evaluation

Please rate _____ on the following characteristics, one being the worst and ten being the best:

Knowledgeable   10 9 8 7 6 5 4 3 2 1

Friendly/Caring   10 9 8 7 6 5 4 3 2 1

Prepared/Organized 10 9 8 7 6 5 4 3 2 1

Respects others   10 9 8 7 6 5 4 3 2 1

Approachable   10 9 8 7 6 5 4 3 2 1

Goal-oriented   10 9 8 7 6 5 4 3 2 1

Describe _____ overall attitude: in and outside of class.

What have you learned from _____ this year?

I like the following things _____ does:

_____ could improve on the following things:

I would also like to say:

Do You Have Any "Confessions?"

Do you have any teaching stories or anecdotes that you would like to share? Currently, the author is working on a compilation book using the experiences of many different educators from all over the country. If you would like to submit one of your teaching experiences and the lesson you learned from it, please send it to:

teacherconfessions@yahoo.com

or

P.O. Box 1809
Waukesha, WI 53187